The *The* **World**

Sports Science
Training Workbook

Editor

Brian Mackenzie

The World
Sports Science
Training Workbook

Editor
Brian Mackenzie

**PEAK
PERFORMANCE**

© Peak Performance Publishing 2004
Reprinted 2005

All rights reserved. No part of this publication may be reproduced,
stored in a retrieval system, or transmitted in any form or by any
means, electronic, mechanical, photocopying, recording or otherwise
without the permission of the publisher.

The information contained in this publication is believed to be correct
at the time of going to press. Whilst care has been taken to ensure that
the information is accurate, the publisher can accept no responsibility
for the consequences of actions based on the advice contained herein.

A CIP catalogue record for this book is available from the British
Library.

Printed by:
PLP Printers
3-7 Mowlem Street
London E2 9HE

Designed by:
Character Design
Highridge
Lower Wrigglebrook Lane
Kingsthorne
Hereford HR2 8AW
Tel: 01981 541154

Published by:
Peak Performance Publishing

Peak Performance Publishing is a trading name of Electric Word plc
Registered office:
67-71 Goswell Road
London
EC1V 7EP
Tel: 0845 450 6402
Website: www.pponline.co.uk

Registered number: 3934419

ISBN: 1-905096-03-8

The World Sports Science Training Workbook

Your one-stop action guide

The World Sports Science Training Workbook was launched to fill a crucial gap in the provision of training advice for athletes and sportspeople.

On the following pages you will find evidence-based advice which is the result of millions of dollars' worth of trials conducted by dedicated sports scientists, with comprehensive, science-based workouts designed for your sport or event. Exercise programmes are displayed in modular format so you can immediately utilise the relevant workout for your sport. Both coaches and athletes will find practical, relevant advice here.

Once under way, your new exercises should help you move quickly up to a higher competitive level. You should also save time as you drop those redundant aspects of training they replace.

As a long-time UK athletics coach, I have always been aware that advice at this level has been expensive and often difficult to obtain. I'm delighted to say this training workbook has solved the twin problems of cost and inconvenience in obtaining expert coaching guidance.

Best wishes

Brian Mackenzie
Editor
brian@brianmac.demon.co.uk

Contents

Module 1

Planning

Introduction

It is often said that planning training programmes is a combination of art and science. One of the most important aspects of sports performance is the athlete being in the best shape at the right time. This is the case not only for the elite athlete arriving at major games or championships, but also for the club athlete aiming for a special event. Athletes will always want to produce personal bests at the events that are most important to them, but to be able to do this the element of risk has to be removed by yearly planning.

Various systems of planning the athlete's year have developed over recent decades, most of which are formed around picking a key event much in advance and working towards such a goal. The event chosen will vary according to the athlete's standard. For the very best, this will indeed be a major championship. For those less confident, it may be the selection race for such a championship, while for those on the level below, it could be a county championships or even a club event. Once the main event is chosen, the athlete should start the planning process by working backwards. The structure of the year can then be completed.

One of the most common methods of structuring the athlete's year is by using the process of periodisation. This involves splitting the year up into a number of periods, which themselves may be sub-divided, with various sections of the training process worked on in each particular period. The generalised pattern used is: preparation, competition and then transition. By splitting the year up into broad phases, not only does this help the planning of a peak for one particular year but it should also ensure a progressive development over a series of years, so an athlete may reach an ultimate sporting target.

Overview of the planning module

Exactly how the year is divided can depend on a variety of factors, ranging from when competitions are to how long it may take for an athlete to peak. In this module we look at how to prepare a training programme to meet your objectives.

- Brian Mackenzie identifies the data that you need to collect and how to prepare a training plan to meet your needs.
- Bruce Tulloh looks at how to plan the year for one season, two seasons, three seasons and all-year-round sports.
- Raphael Brandon looks at how to design a sport-specific fitness programme.
- Daniel Bishop provides a blueprint for a self-determined training programme to enhance your feelings of competence in your sport.

The articles in this module are applicable to most sports.

Planning your training is essential – here is how to do it

The detailed planning of an athlete's training programme is essential if both short- and long-term objectives are to be achieved at the right time in the season.

Training plan

The purpose of a training plan is to identify the work to be carried out to achieve agreed objectives. Training plans should be drawn up to identify long-term (say, four years) objectives as well as short-term plans for the forthcoming season. For the rest of this topic I will concentrate on the development of the short-term annual training plan. In its simplest form the plan could comprise a single A4 sheet identifying the overall plan for the year and more detailed weekly plans identifying the specific activities the athlete is to carry out.

Training year

The start of the training year will depend upon the athlete's circumstances and objectives, but this would generally be around October for track and field athletics in the UK.

Information-gathering

The first stage of preparing a training plan is to gather background information about your athlete and their objectives for the forthcoming season. The sort of information to collect is as follows:

Personal details

- name, address, date of birth, telephone numbers, transport arrangements
- objectives
- performance (time, height, distance)
- technical (development of event technique)
- indoor and/or outdoor season
- experience
- personal best (PBs)
- competition experience (club, county, national, country).

Equipment

- does the athlete have their own equipment?
- harness and tyre
- elastic harness
- weight jackets
- camcorder
- distance, time, percentage-effort matrix.

Finance

- where can grants be obtained from?

Competition

- date of main competition
- national and area championships
- school, university competitions
- required qualification times for competitions
- fixture lists – club, county, country etc
- open meetings.

Competitors

- who are the competition and what are their personal bests (PBs)?
- recent competition results
- competition behaviour.

Athlete's other commitments

- school, college, work, part-time jobs
- family and partner
- hobbies and other sports
- time available for training
- planned holidays.

Medical

- previous injuries or illness
- current problems (eg diabetes, asthma etc)
- access to medical support
- physiotherapy support
- on any medication – is it a banned substance?
- using asthma inhaler – application to use Beta 2 agent inhalers.

Training facilities

- tracks and other running facilities (bad weather)
- gymnasiums and weight training
- swimming pools, saunas and massage
- coaching workshops.

Last season

- what can be learned from last season?

Key questions for the athlete

- how serious are you about your sport?
- what do expect from your coach?

Periodisation

Periodisation is the method of organising the training year into phases where each phase has its specific aims for the athlete's development.

The phases of a training year

The training year should be divided into phases
- Phase 1 – 16 weeks – Oct, Nov, Dec, Jan
- Phase 2 – 8 weeks – Feb, Mar
- Phase 3 – 8 weeks – Apr, May
- Phase 4 – 8 weeks – Jun, mid-Jul
- Phase 5 – 8 weeks – mid-Jul, Aug
- Phase 6 – 4 weeks – Sep

This assumes that the competition climax will be in August (Phase 5).

What if there is an indoor and an outdoor season?

For the athlete with competitive objectives for both the indoor and outdoor season, the phase allocation for the indoor season could be as follows:
- Phase 1 – 6 weeks – Oct, mid-Nov

- Phase 2 – 8 weeks – mid-Nov, Dec, mid-Jan
- Phase 3 – 6 weeks – mid-Jan, Feb

and the outdoor season as follows:
- Phase 1 – 4 weeks – Feb, mid-Mar
- Phase 2 – 6 weeks – mid-Mar, mid-Apr
- Phase 3 – 5 weeks – mid-Apr, May
- Phase 4 – 7 weeks – Jun, mid-Jul
- Phase 5 – 6 weeks – mid-Jul, Aug
- Phase 6 – 4 weeks – Sep

This assumes that the climax of the indoor season is in February and the outdoor season in August. Depending on your athlete's objectives and abilities, the year start and duration of each phase may have to be adjusted to achieve appropriate development.

Objectives of each phase

The objectives of each phase are as follows:
- Phase 1 – General development of strength, mobility, endurance and basic technique
- Phase 2 – Development of specific fitness and advanced technical skills
- Phase 3 – Competition experience – achievement of indoor objectives
- Phase 4 – Adjustment of technical model, preparation for the main competition
- Phase 5 – Competition experience and achievement of outdoor objectives
- Phase 6 – Active recovery – planning preparation for next season.

Activities conducted in each phase of training

The athlete's physical needs that require development are:
- basic body conditioning (including balance, coordination and core stability)
- general and specific strength
- general and specific technique
- general and specific mobility
- general and specific endurance
- speed.

Each of these needs is a building block, where specific blocks need to be in place before you progress to the next. Failure to do this may result in injury. How you allocate the blocks to each phase depends upon the athlete's weaknesses and strengths and is for the coach to decide with the athlete.

One approach is to progress the building blocks as follows:
- basic body conditioning
- general strength, endurance, mobility and technique

- specific strength, endurance, mobility and technique
- speed.

When progressing from one block to the next, remember to fade one out as the other comes in, and not to switch from one block to the next overnight. Some blocks once started may continue to the end of the season, but at a less intense level, *eg* mobility. Other blocks to consider are relaxation, visualisation and psychology (mental attitude).

Preparing a plan

The steps in producing a training plan are as follows:

Produce an overall plan template and identify the months/weeks of the year

Identify on the plan at the appropriate period:
- the main competition
- area, national, school etc championships
- qualification competitions
- club fixture meetings
- the six phases based on the main competition in Phase 5.

Identify on the plan:
- the blocks (*eg* strength, endurance) to be developed in each phase
- the period of development for each block
- the intensity of training week by week
- number of training sessions per week
- evaluation points to monitor progress.

Identify appropriate training units for each block as appropriate to the phase of development.

Group the training units for each block into training schedules taking into consideration:
- the number of training sessions the athlete can complete per week
- the required training intensity
- the phase of development.

What are a training unit and a training session?

A training unit is a single activity (*eg* 6 x 60m at 90 to 95% effort with two minutes' recovery) with a set objective (*eg* develop speed endurance). A training session is made up of one or more training units, *eg* warm-up unit, technique drills unit, speed endurance unit and a cool-down unit.

What is a training schedule?

A training schedule (microcycle) comprises a number of training units that can span from seven to 30 days.

What are a microcycle, mesocycle and macrocycle?

A microcycle, also known as a training schedule, is a group of training units. The mesocycle, also known as a macrocycle, is a number of repeats of a microcycle.

Goal-setting

Goal-setting is a simple, yet often misused, motivational technique which can provide some structure for your training and competition programme. Goals give a focus and there are two well-known acronyms to guide goal-setting:

SMART or SMARTER

    S – goals must be **Specific**
    M – training targets should be **Measurable**
    A – goals should be **Adjustable**
    R – goals must be **Realistic**
    T – training targets should be **Time**-based
    E – goals should be challenging and **Exciting**
    R – goals should be **Recorded**.

We'll see how this is put into action later on in this module.

SCCAMP

    S – goals must be **Specific**
    C – within the **Control** of the athlete
    C – goals are **Challenging**
    A – goals must be **Attainable**
    M – training targets should be **Measurable**
    P – goals are **Personal**.

FITT principles

The basic principles of fitness training are summed up in the acronym FITT.
    F – **Frequency** – How often?
    I – **Intensity** – How hard?
    T – **Time** – How long?
    T – **Type** – the type of training (strength, endurance etc).

Summary

The training plans for my athletes are based on the six phases discussed above, where each phase comprises a repeated four-week training schedule (microcycle). The workload in the first three weeks of the four-week programme increases each week (easy, medium and hard) and the fourth week comprises active recovery and tests to monitor training progress. The aim of the four-week cycle is:

- to build you up to a level of fitness (three weeks)
- test, recovery and adjustment of the training programme (one week)
- to build you up to higher level of fitness (three weeks)
- test, recovery and adjustment of the training programme (one week)
- to build you up to an even higher level of fitness (three weeks).

The content and quantity of training in each week and phase will depend on many factors. Remember a training programme is athlete-specific and the results of the tests in the fourth week can be used to adjust the training in the next four-week cycle to address any limitations.

Brian Mackenzie

Planning the year – overview

Periodisation means 'dividing a season or a year into separate periods'. It follows from this that within each period or phase there are different objectives. I prefer to use the word 'phase' because it fits the concept better. 'Periods' are thought of as having precisely fixed timescales, like school periods, where as phases are usually thought of as transitional, things which one moves through. One phase merges into another and this is what should happen with a properly organised training programme.

The one-season sport

If your sport is a 'summer only' sport, such as rowing or cricket, the phasing takes care of itself. The competitive season, from May to September, is followed by a break (say, of one month). There is then a 'basic fitness' or 'maintenance' phase that might last until February. This is followed by the 'build-up phase' and the 'pre-competition phase'. With a winter sport such as rugby there will be a six-month competitive season, and with football there may be an eight-month season. The long competitive season poses a particular problem, one that has no satisfactory solution, but this article may help to clarify the coach's thoughts.

Two-season sports

British distance runners usually have a track season, from May to September, and a cross-country season that runs until March and may start in October. To this, one must add road relay competition in spring and autumn, indoor racing in winter, and the never-ending season of road racing. The current decline in British distance running standards, in spite of increasing numbers of participants, may well be attributable to the surfeit of competition, which makes phasing more difficult. The sportsperson who spends the European winter competing in Australia or the person who plays tennis in the summer and squash in the winter is in the same position.

Three-season sports

It might be better to speak of 'three-peak' sports here: a rugby player who has a pre-Christmas peak, a Sevens tournament at Easter and an overseas tour in August, or a distance runner who runs 10,000m on the track in the summer, a marathon in the autumn, and cross-country from January to March.

All-year-round sports

The majority of road-runners come into this category, as do those who have reached international level in golf or tennis.

The problem

The difficulty is that the human body cannot tolerate a high stress level indefinitely. When a small amount of stress is imposed, the body responds. Hormones are produced which raise the level of performance and speed up the rate of recovery. If the stress increases, the body responds yet again, but if the stress persists at a high level the system will eventually 'crash', leading to the over-training syndrome described by Dr Richard Budget (*BMJ*, vol 309, 13 August 1994). The obvious signs of this are:

- loss of performance
- depression and irritability
- disturbed sleep pattern
- increased resting pulse rate
- loss of weight
- frequent minor infections.

When the training and competition regime is being worked out, remember that the body responds to the total stress load, not just to the stress of training and competition. Thus, if the athlete is getting married, taking important exams or moving house (or all three at once), they should not be subjected to the normal amount of training stress. Competition should either be deferred or restricted.

The next thing to bear in mind is that competition and hard training are destructive processes. Muscle cells are damaged, electrolytes are leaked, glycogen stores are depleted, blood cells are destroyed, and in contact sports the damage may be even more severe. The rate of recovery from the hard work is an individual thing and even the fittest full-time athlete cannot train hard every day.

On the other hand, most athletes are a long way from reaching their full fitness potential. A top-class distance runner can put in three running sessions a day, totalling over 120 miles (200K) per week, plus two swims and a gym workout, and the athlete can maintain this for weeks on end, if carefully supervised. Contrast this with the club rugby player who complains that they are too tired from their weekend match to train two evenings a week.

The solution

If we think of the body as a machine, then there should be at least one time of the year when we take the whole thing to pieces, replace or strengthen the worn-out parts, oil it, protect it, put it together again and test it. For the human body, this involves analysing the sport and deciding which parts really need building up and which can be left to repair themselves.

The resting phase

Proper rest is vital and must be programmed into each day, week and phase of the year. But in addition there should be a resting phase, if only a brief one, at the end of each competitive phase. During this time the stress level should be at its lowest, enabling the anti-stress system to regenerate. This does not mean that physical exercise should stop; I am convinced that it should not, but that there should be a complete change of routine. The rower should get out of their boat, the footballer should go fishing, the runner should go walking and the walker should get on their bike. Two to four weeks of this will probably be enough.

The basic fitness phase

Here, as far as possible, one should be training the whole body, but even so there will be differences between sports. Those who rely more on muscle strength will spend more time on weight training, while others will devote more time to flexibility, to endurance or to oxygen uptake, but any serious athlete should be covering all these fields, because without them they will not be fully fit and will thus be less able to meet the demands of the hard pre-competition phase.

If the athlete is trying to improve from the previous season, they will have to get used to putting in more hours per week. It makes sense to increase the volume of the training first and then to gradually introduce training of a higher intensity, first one hard session a week, then two. The length of this phase is really governed by the time which needs to be spent on the next, most vital, phase.

Pre-competition training

Training is specific to the event. It is no good being the best at training four hours a day if you cannot produce your best in the competition, so you need to analyse the demands of the competition. The runner is getting ready for a race that might last for less than four minutes (a mile), less than 14 minutes (5000m) or over two hours (a marathon). A footballer (any kind) has to be fit for intense 10-second bursts of running and for brief but extreme exertions of strength, but they must also be able to cope with spending 90 minutes or more on their feet at a time, maintaining their mental and physical agility under conditions of great stress. Their training programme must therefore include a lot of endurance work as well as skill, speed and strength training.

Hard training is most effective if one can train different elements on different days, or at different times of day. Adding a training load to an already tired body is a recipe for disaster and the coach must choose the right balance of rest and exercise. In the beginning, 'little and often' is a much better way of building up fitness than the 'train till you drop' method.

At a low level one might start with one hard and three easy sessions a week, with the hard day being similar to the competition but less intense. In the easy sessions the athlete could incorporate different elements of the necessary training, one day long and slow for endurance, one day with some leg speed training, one day in the gym for strength and flexibility.

A year later the same athlete might be doing six sessions a week, two hard and four easy, and a couple of years further down the road they might be doing 12 sessions a week, six for endurance and recuperation, three for hard event-specific training, and three others for minor elements such as speed or flexibility. An example of an event-specific workout might be 4 x 3k for a marathon runner, while for a footballer it might be a circuit of sprints and drills with short recovery breaks.

As the competition season approaches, one tries to integrate all the different aspects of training. The total training load is reduced and the hard training sessions come closer to simulating the competition conditions, but they are spaced out by longer recovery intervals. Practice games and trials lead into the next phase.

The competitive phase

This is not as simple as it seems. If one did nothing but compete and recover from competition, the performance level would soon flatten out and then start to drop. In my view it is hard to perform consistently at a high level for more than six weeks without a break. There should be some sort of 'refresher course' after six weeks. This can be done either for the whole team, or, if the programme does not allow for a break, certain members of the squad should be taken out and put through a mini-cycle of training before going back into competition.

During competition, there must be some training to maintain the basic strong points. The runner must preserve their aerobic fitness and endurance; therefore their total mileage must not drop too much. The 'explosive' athlete must maintain their strength levels, so time must be found for strength training.

Monitoring

The coach has to keep a close eye out to spot the signs of over-training or over-competing as soon as they start to occur. Keeping a daily check on the athlete's resting pulse and body weight will give a good indication and getting either the athlete or the coach to keep a diary recording the athlete's response to each session is even more revealing. The more the coach is aware of the athlete's condition, the more likely the athlete is to keep fit through a long season. The athlete must try to control the environment so that stress does not become too great. Above all, the athlete must realise that if there are to be peaks in a sportsperson's life, there must also be troughs.

Bruce Tulloh

How to design a sport-specific fitness programme

The fitness trainer is now becoming accepted as a necessary member of the modern coaching team. This new coaching model has the head coach leading a team of specialist coaches, therapists and sports scientists. For example, a secondary technical coach, a physiotherapist, a psychologist, a fitness trainer and a physiologist accompany the head coach, with each performing their specified role, but communicating and working as a team.

For elite sports, the trainer should be able to design workouts that cover all relevant fitness areas: strength, flexibility, agility, aerobic and anaerobic endurance and speed. These workouts must be both specific to the sport and suitable for the level of the athlete. In addition, the trainer should be able to assess fitness levels, understand physiological and biomechanical test data, liaise with physiotherapists regarding injury prevention and rehabilitation, and also be able to pass on sound nutritional instruction. This job description, if carried out to full capacity, requires a great deal of expertise and experience and is likely to be beyond the knowledge base of most head coaches. Thus, the advantage of using a specialist fitness trainer is that they have the specific skills, experience and time to optimise the physical preparation of the athlete.

The purpose of this section is to explain the principles behind designing a sport-specific fitness programme and describe some of the important training methods that should be employed. Specifically I will discuss fitness assessment procedures, and analyse the fitness demands of a sport: strength and power training, balance and stability training, endurance training, and speed and agility training.

Fitness assessment and needs analysis

The principles behind designing sports training programmes are analogous to the methods used by corporate management consultancy firms. When asked to provide a business solution, a management consultancy firm will begin by establishing the goal the client wants to achieve. They then assess the client's current status, systems, markets, etc. The final step is to calculate what is required to bridge the gap between the client's current status and what they need to achieve their business goal. This final step is called gap analysis. The plan they implement is based completely on the outcome of the gap analysis.

This gap analysis model is exactly how a sports fitness programme should be designed:
- Step 1 is to set the athlete's or team's goals: what do they want to achieve?
- Step 2 is to assess the athlete's or team's current level of fitness. This assessment must cover the entire relevant fitness areas specific to their sport or event.
- Step 3 is the gap analysis, which is calculating the difference for each fitness component between the current and ideal fitness levels.
- Step 4 is designing the training programme that will improve each respective fitness area to the required level.

This example should clarify the situation

Player profile: Male 19 year-old national tennis player. Some weight training experience and completes regular cycling and treadmill workouts.

1. Goal – to become a professional player on tour
2. Establish fitness status

Test	Fitness area	Current	Ideal
Multi-stage fitness test	Aerobic	VO$_2$max = 52	VO$_2$max = 55
30m sprint	Speed	4.2 sec	3.9 sec
Standing long jump	Leg power	2.3m	2.8m
Overhead medicine ball throw	Arm power	16.1m	16m
20m shuttle run	Agility	4.7 sec	<4.5 sec

Gap analysis

Aerobic fitness is pretty good – not far off ideal. All the sprint, agility and leg power tests are below ideal, especially the standing long jump test, suggesting that leg power could be improved. Arm power is fine and therefore needs only to be maintained.

The programme

The player has a six-week period of no competitive tennis so we will devise a plan to improve leg power and agility for this period, while maintaining upper body strength and aerobic fitness.

Monday	Frappier drills, squat jumps, standing long jumps, hexagon drill, lateral hops
	Resisted sprints, 10 x T drill, two minutes' rest
Tuesday	Power cleans, squats, leg curls, power lunges, medicine ball for upper body and trunk
Wednesday	As Monday
Thursday	Easy aerobic session plus medicine ball work
Friday	Rest
Saturday	As Monday

The progression over six weeks would be to increase the intensity of the drills and the weights lifted in the gym, *eg* replace squat jumps with drop jumps into lateral sprint. By the end of the six-week period the player would be re-tested and hopefully we would see improvements in 30m sprint, standing long jump test and 20m shuttle run test.

The training programme

The assessment results are analysed to establish which fitness areas need to be developed to raise competitive performance. The design of the training programme should prioritise these areas to bring them up to scratch. The fitness areas that are already good can simply be maintained. This principle recognises the fact that it is difficult to develop all aspects of physical performance at once. This is because of both practical issues (there may be simply a lack of time to work on all areas during the training week) and physiological issues (in that endurance training compromises strength and power development). The following sections will briefly describe appropriate training methods and their dosage for each of the fitness aspects.

Strength and power

At some stage every athlete needs to develop strength and power. The best results are achieved by training two to four times a week, with little concurrent endurance training. In competitive periods, this is not practical for many sports, although research has shown strength maintenance and sometimes improvements, are possible through a season with regular strength training. The best solution is for strength and power development to be planned for the off-season and then maintained through the season.

To develop maximum strength, a weights exercise session should be designed. A typical session comprises five to 10 exercises with two to four sets of five to 12 repetitions maximum (RM) per exercise. To develop power, plyometric exercises are most commonly used. A session comprises five to eight exercises with a total of 100 to 300 foot/shoulder contacts per workout, depending on the athlete's level and time of year. Weights and plyometric exercises can be combined in the same session. This is called complex training and is very effective for peaking.

Always choose weights and plyometric exercises that are functional to the sport or movement. For example, squats and drop jumps are better for vertical jumping ability than power lunges and standing long jumps, which are better for horizontal jumping or sprints. For another example, choose free weights instead of machines as synergistic muscles are involved to stabilise. Think about the type of contractions involved in the sports movements – *eg* hamstrings' eccentric function – the joint angle and the speeds of movements.

Sometimes upper body strength is incorrectly overemphasised. For instance, in tennis upper-body power training is more important, as a racquet only weighs 400 grams. If your 1RM squat is not significantly more than your 1RM bench press, then you have been doing too much upper-body work in the gym.

Aerobic endurance

Aerobic fitness is primary for most sports. However, it is not the only fitness area and if it is focused on too much, it can be detrimental to strength and power which are equally, if not more, important in many sports. Trainers must think carefully about the fitness level they believe is appropriate for peak performance and then achieve that. For example, in elite football a high aerobic capacity is important, but for volleyball a moderate level will suffice. For most games, aerobic fitness governs how quickly one recovers between high-intensity sections and how much distance can be covered in a game.

Anaerobic endurance

Anaerobic endurance is also important for many sports. This is the ability to work at a high intensity repeatedly. Both the lactate system and the adenosine triphosphate-phosphate creatine (ATP-PC) system should be trained (more about these in a later module), but targeted in the correct proportions for each sport. For instance, tennis focuses almost solely on the ATP-PC system, due to short bursts and the frequent rest-play pattern, whereas squash requires significant lactate system training as it is much more continuous. Anaerobic endurance can be developed with training two to three times a week.

Speed and agility

Speed and agility are key to many sports but often in very different ways, each sport having its own particular demands. For instance, fencing requires very quick footwork and acceleration but all movements are linear – forwards and backwards. In contrast, racquet sports are multidirectional, with as much lateral movement as linear.

In addition, different sports have different speed profiles. Racquet sports require very fast off-the-mark acceleration, but maximum speed over a longer sprint of 30 to 60m is less important. Rugby and football require both good acceleration and maximum speed. Therefore maximum speed and acceleration need to be differentiated in training.

Speed training sessions must always include long rest periods and focus solely on quality. Speed development is about teaching the neuro-muscular system to operate at full speed and power and this is not possible if there is any fatigue. If rests are too short, the training will only develop speed endurance and not maximum speed.

Balance, coordination and stability

A final area that must be incorporated into a sports training programme is balance, coordination and stability training. Economy of movement, peak power and agility cannot be optimised unless the athlete has highly developed balance and stability.

Balance and coordination have to be developed through many different methods as variety is important. Exercises on the wobble board and balance beam are great for this. With a little imagination one can think of many things to challenge an athlete's balance and coordination, *eg* balancing on a wobble board while juggling.

Stability, especially in the trunk, must also be developed through various methods. I recommend using gymnastic balls and learning some Tai Chi moves, as well as using a medicine ball for the stomach and lower back exercises. Particularly effective are static bridging exercises, *eg* the plank, for developing functional core stability. A stability workout should be performed at least twice a week.

Raphael Brandon

How to design a self-determined training programme that will drive you to new heights

Have you ever stopped to wonder why some individuals stick with a structured training schedule while others give up at the first obstacle? Or why, three months into your perfectly planned programme, your enthusiasm dwindles? The reasons for some people's persistence in following an exercise programme have been researched for many years, with no conclusive answers (see Dishman, 1993, for a review).

Among the proposed explanations, to name but a few, are: the attributes of the individual, their occupation, biomedical status, environmental factors and time. The complex and rich phenomenon that affects all of these to some degree is motivation. As you may know, Deci and Ryan in 1985 proposed their Cognitive Evaluation Theory, which posits that intrinsic motivation is maximised when individuals feel competent and self-determining when dealing with their environment.

For you as the dedicated exerciser, this means that you have some control over the content of your exercise programme and its outcomes, rather than being dictated to by the schedule itself. Intrinsic motivation means simply the reasons for taking part in a particular activity – in our case, physical conditioning for peak performance – which come from inside the individual. More specifically, intrinsically motivated athletes participate because they find the activity inherently enjoyable, rather than for external rewards, *eg* coach recognition, which is called extrinsic motivation.

I am going to provide you with your own blueprint for a self-determined training programme to enhance your feelings of competence in your sport. In turn, the programme will provide the motivational push you may need in order to achieve your particular goals. Along the way, I will combine proven theoretical material with some of my own practical knowledge to enable you to motivate yourself to levels you did not think possible.

Goal-setting: get SMART

Goal-setting is a simple, yet often misused, motivational technique which can provide some structure for your training and competition programme. Goals give a focus and the key to effective goal-setting is the SMART principle.

a) First, goals must be **Specific**. Research has shown (Locke and Latham, 1990) that specific goals work better than general 'do your best' goals. For example, if you are a runner, rather than professing a desire to reduce your 5k time, you should state: 'I intend to knock 20 seconds off my 5k time over the next six months'.

b) Your training target ought to be **Measurable**, as in the above example. Simply saying that you want to trim your 5k time is insufficient; you need some accurate means of charting your progress. This means that continuous monitoring is needed, but this can become a bore. Thus I would recommend that you build into your training schedule a regular 'measurement day' on which you test yourself in various disciplines. This can take place once a week or even once a month, but the idea of the day is to reduce your preoccupation with times and improvement. Certainly, the therapeutic benefits arising from a relaxed (non-timed) workout can help to alleviate stress, reduce symptoms of depression and leave you ready to proceed with an otherwise arduous training schedule (see Morgan, WP, Ed, 1997, for coverage of the physical activity and mental health literature).

c) Goals should also be **Adjustable**. Goal-setting is a dynamic process. If, for instance, you become injured during a competitive season, you should be able to lower your targets accordingly. On the other hand, you may make such rapid progress that you can raise them. Ultimately this means that they must conform to the first two criteria: being specific and measurable.

d) Goals must be **Realistic**. It is all very well saying 'I want to break Daniel Komen's 5k record', but unless you are his (as yet, undiscovered) identical twin, then that does not seem a realistic goal. This is an extreme example, but you also must recognise that your room for improvement shrinks as you get near your full potential – the well-known Law of Diminishing Returns. Conversely, goals should be difficult enough so that you are not struck down by acute boredom because you have achieved them too easily.

e) Finally, your training targets ought to be **Time**-based. If you do not give yourself a specific time frame in which the goal must be achieved, the urgency for attainment is reduced. The previous example of trimming the 5k time by 20 seconds within six months satisfies this criterion. Try to resist the temptation to move these time constraints back to accommodate life events, such as minor injuries; the result is that the value of the time limit is negated. It is important to identify when this happens, and to set about designing new objectives with new time parameters. This way your goal-setting plan will not lose its effectiveness.

Make no mistake about it – goal-setting is a skill that needs to be mastered just like any other. But by using the following model, you can make the process a little less taxing.

The interval goal-setting model

The interval goal-setting (IGS) model was devised by Frank O'Block and Frederick Evans in the early 1980s to provide a quantifiable means of setting training targets. The model was developed in order to help coaches and athletes set more realistic and achievable goals and it takes into consideration the athlete's past five performances when determining their target performances. It embodies most of the fundamentals of SMART goal-setting. I will guide you through the requisite steps so you need to make a minimum of effort.

First, sit down and establish one or more long-term goals for yourself, using the SMART principle of goal-setting: where do you want to be in, say, a year's time? What competition do you wish to do well in? Or what long-term personal achievements do you consider to be crucial to your sense of accomplishment? Any effective goal-setting plan consists of three main types of goal: long-term, intermediate and short-term. If your long-term aim is in one year from the start of your training, then intermediate goals could be between two and nine months, and short-term within eight weeks. The IGS model works most effectively for short-term goals.

The following variables are required in the IGS model computation:

A = your average time over the last five performances

B = your best time within the last five performances

C = the difference between your average and best performances (A - B)

D = the lower boundary of your target interval

E = the interval midpoint

F = the upper boundary of the target interval.

For example

Here is how to utilise the IGS model for a 5k run time:

a) Record your five last performance times – 16:47, 16:55, 16:44, 16:46, 16:52

b) Find A, the average of the five times = 16:49

c) Find B, the best time from the five performances = 16:44

d) Find C, the difference between your average (A) and your best time (B)

$C = A - B$

$C = 16:49 - 16:44$

$C = 0:05$

e) Find D, the lower boundary of the interval, or the best time you recorded – for this example it is B, so D = 16:44

f) Find E, the interval midpoint

$E = D - C$

$E = 16:44 - 0:05$

$E = 16:39$

g) Find F, the interval upper boundary

$F = E - C$

$F = 16:39 - 0:05$

$F = 16:34$

What it all means

You now possess a collection of figures that represents your target interval. In order to clarify the computation results, you can show the model graphically. Draw a horizontal line 10cm in length; mark your average and the upper boundary as 1cm vertical lines at the right and left ends respectively, so that a reduction in time is represented by a shift along the scale from left to right. At a point 2.5cm from the left end of your line (your average time), mark another vertical line for your previous best; this forms the lower boundary of your target interval. At the halfway point along the continuum, you should draw another vertical line, to represent the midpoint of the interval.

What this shows is that the interval midpoint is realistically higher than your previous best, by as much as your previous best exceeded your average. The upper boundary of the interval is to allow for particularly exceptional performance. In the example above, a reduction in time of 10 seconds from the previous best time is quite considerable, corresponding approximately to a reduction from 5:23 per mile pace to 5:20. While this may seem only a measly abatement, let us not forget that this corresponds to a difference in performance from one week to the next!

Modifying the model

Subsequent IGS increments can be computed with each new performance after the sixth has been recorded, to ensure that fresh dynamic targets are continually being set. All you need to do to find the next interval target is to discard the previous first time from the analysis and include the sixth. This is repeated every time a new time trial is recorded. I recommend that you pin up the IGS model in a prominent place so your family and friends can see it. Publicly declared intentions are more likely to be stuck to than those kept hidden. I have made a sheet covered in sticky-backed plastic, which acts as a wipe off model, so I can renew my targets frequently.

To modify the IGS model to allow for increases in performance scores, such as those encountered in progressive weight training, make the following adjustments: C becomes B - A, E becomes D + C and F becomes E + C.

When carrying out the graphical computations, the only adjustment you need to make is to reverse the sum for each of parts A, C and D. For example: F - A instead of A - F.

Keeping SCORE with rewards

Perhaps you act as a coach, exercise leader or in a similar capacity. One primary role of the coach is as a motivator and another useful goal-setting tool for the coach is that of token rewards. These can influence performance without a goal-setting programme, or vice versa. However, when the two are used in conjunction, the possibility of performance enhancement is increased (Locke, Shaw, Saari and Latham, 1981). The word 'token' is important because the rewards must not have any real value or worth for the athlete or their motivation will ultimately be undermined. Deci (1971) explained two further salient aspects of rewards, namely that they can be 'controlling' or 'informational'.

If the controlling aspect of any reward is considered to be overly important by the athlete, their levels of motivation will decrease, since they perceive the coach to be externally manipulating their performances. If, however, they perceive the reward as purely informative, the reward will affect their perception of their own competence. If the information implies ability, intrinsic motivation will increase. If it implies a lack of ability, then intrinsic motivation will decline. Bearing this in mind, the successful coach will follow the SCORE guidelines:

- **Simple.** Choose a reward system that can be easily implemented, such as points, rather than major items, *eg* medals. The athlete can then accumulate a score for periodic evaluation.

- **Consistent**. Be consistent when giving out rewards and consistently target behaviours such as a performance landing within a target interval of the IGS model.

- **Observable**. Pick target behaviours that can be easily evaluated, such as those encountered in the SMART programme.

- **Reachable**. Make sure that you choose to reward behaviours that are not comparative, ie they should not be dependent on the performance of others. To use sport psychology language, use rewards to encourage your athletes to strive for 'performance' or 'process' goals rather than 'outcome' goals (Duda, 1992). Performance goals are concerned with improvement in relation to one's own previous best performance, such as in the IGS model. Process goals focus on the aspects the athlete has to work on in order to succeed in attaining their ultimate aim, *eg* a swimmer focusing on an increased arm reach in order to improve their swimming economy. Outcome goals are primarily concerned with winning. If coaches continually stress these goals, their athletes are headed for disappointment because of an inevitable dependence on the performance of others. Even the very best athletes, at the top of their sport, however much they aspire to win, set themselves performance and process goals in training.

- **Explanation**. Finally, explain to your athlete at the beginning of any particular training session (maybe a 'measurement' day) the targets to be rewarded. For instance, 'one point will be accredited to anyone performing above their average, two points to anyone reaching the target interval, three for above the midpoint...' etc. Athletes who do not perform to the specified levels go unrewarded. This is referred to as 'contingency management'.

The two acronyms that I have used in this article, SMART and SCORE, will go a long way towards ensuring that your training programme, when combined with the IGS model, develops near maximum effectiveness. You may have noticed that they both rely on the emergence of various successes along the road to peak performance. These successes develop an overall perception of individual competence, which brings me to my final point.

A word about 'self-efficacy'

Self-efficacy (SE) (see Bandura, 1977 and 1986) represents the belief that one can successfully negotiate a chosen course of action, such as the execution of a particular sports skill. It can be described as a kind of situation-specific self-confidence. People with high SE participate more readily, work harder, persist longer when they encounter difficulties and achieve at a higher level. In short, they are more motivated (Schunk, 1995). The general principles of effective goal-setting must be adhered to, *ie* SMART goal-setting with constant feedback (perhaps in the shape of rewards), in order for efficacy beliefs to be enhanced and maintained. SE arises from a range of sources, which I have listed here in descending order of importance.

- Past performance accomplishments. If an athlete continually experiences success in an activity, within the constraints of the training programme, they will feel more able to perform that activity. Past performances are reckoned by Bandura to have a reciprocal relationship with SE. In other words, not only do past accomplishments induce greater SE, but also a greater sense of SE can affect the person's subsequent performance.
- Vicarious experience. This means seeing other people, most often peers, successfully reaching a target, thus instigating a feeling of 'If they can do it, so can I!' This suggests that it makes sense to surround yourself with people whom you consider to be similar to yourself in terms of build, age, ability, etc so that realistic positive role models abound. Obviously this could be achieved by joining a suitable club.
- Verbal persuasion. This is a mildly effective method of inducing SE, and can easily be implemented by coaches and team mates. However, verbal persuasion is reckoned to have greater impact when it comes from someone who is perceived as a trusted and credible source of information. Feltz (1992) also considers self-talk and imagery to be forms of persuasion.
- The athlete's 'psychological arousal' is also regarded by Bandura as a factor in determining their sense of efficacy. Heightened physiological signals such as elevated heart rate are sometimes interpreted as signs of anxiety, leading to a preoccupation with them that can damage performance.

Finally, the concepts of goal-setting and rewards can be incorporated into a holistic perception of competence, namely global self-efficacy. A SMART programme sets out difficult but attainable goals. Consequently, efficacy perceptions should increase as successive targets/objectives are reached. Similarly, the token rewards that the coach gives for desirable behaviour or performance can become tangible evidence of competence in the goal-setting programme. Use the techniques highlighted in this article and stick to their guidelines and I can guarantee that your training will motivate you to new heights.

Daniel Bishop

References

Bandura, A (1977),
'Self-efficacy: toward a unifying theory of behaviour change'.
Psychological Review, 84, pp191-215

Bandura, A (1986), *Social foundations of thought and action.* Englewood Cliffs,
NJ: Prentice Hall

Deci, EL (1971), 'Effects of externally mediated rewards on intrinsic motivation'.
Journal of Personality & Social Psychology, 18, pp105-115

Deci, EL, and Ryan, RM (1985), *Intrinsic motivation and self-determination in human behaviour.* New York: Plenum

Dishman, RK (1993), 'Exercise adherence' In Singer, RN, Murphey, M and
Tennant, LK (Eds), *Handbook of Research on Sport Psychology,* pp. 779-798,
New York: Macmillan

Duda, J (1992), 'Motivation in sport settings: a goal perspective approach' In
Roberts, GC (Ed), *Motivation in Sport and Exercise,* pp57-91,
Champaign, IL: Human Kinetics

Feltz, DL (1992), 'Understanding motivation in sport: a self-efficacy perspective'
In Roberts, GC (Ed), *Motivation in Sport and Exercise,* pp93-105,
Champaign, IL: Human Kinetics

Locke, EA, and Latham, GP (1990), *A theory of goal-setting and task performance.*
Englewood Cliffs, NJ: Prentice Hall

Locke, EA, Shaw, KN, Saari, LM, and Latham, GP (1981), 'Goal setting and task
performance: 1969-1980' *Psychological Bulletin,* 90, pp125-152

Morgan WP (Ed) (1997), *Physical activity and mental health.*
Bristol, PA: Taylor & Francis

O'Block, FR, and Evans, FH, 'Goal setting as a motivational technique'
In Silva, JM, and Weinberg, RS (Eds), *Psychological foundations of sport,* pp188-196,
Champaign, IL: Human Kinetics

Schunk, D (1995), 'Self-efficacy, motivation and performance',
Journal of Applied Sport Psychology, 7, pp112-137

Module 2

Injury Prevention

Introduction

Like most athletes, you undoubtedly want to lower your chances of incurring an injury while participating in your favourite sport. Injuries decrease the amount of time you can spend in leisure activities, lower your fitness, downgrade competitive performance and can lead to long-term health problems.

Sports scientists suggest that injury rates could be reduced by 25% if athletes took appropriate preventative action.

Overview of the injury prevention module

There are some general rules for injury avoidance that apply to all sports. In this module we look at how you can reduce the chances of developing a sports injury.

- Brian Mackenzie explains how to assess your potential of being sidelined with an injury and the preventative actions you can take to reduce this.
- Raphael Brandon explains how to reduce your chances of injury by eliminating training errors.
- Dr Simon Kemp and Chris Boynes explain how monitoring muscle imbalance can reduce the chances of injury.
- Bruce Tulloh provides some valuable and practical tips to reduce the chances of injury.
- Brian Mackenzie explains how you can use cryotherapy to treat soft tissue injuries.

The articles in this module are applicable to most sports.

How to avoid injury

Common misconceptions

Many coaches and athletes believe that males have higher injury rates than females. But male and female athletes have about the same injury rate per hour of training. Among runners it is considered that training speed is the cause of injuries ('speed kills') but research indicates that there is no link between speed and injury risk.

Don't overdo it

The amount of training you carry out plays a key role in determining your real injury risk. Studies have shown that your best direct injury predictor may be the amount of training you completed last month. Fatigued muscles do a poor job of protecting their associated connective tissues, increasing the risk of damage to bone, cartilage, tendons and ligaments. If you are a runner, the link between training quantity and injury means that the total mileage is an excellent indicator of your injury risk. The more miles you accrue per week, the higher the chances of injury. One recent investigation found a marked upswing in injury risk above 40 miles of running per week.

The two best predictors of injury

1. If you have been injured before, you are much more likely to get hurt than an athlete who has been injury-free. Regular exercises have a way of uncovering the weak areas of the body. If your knees are put under heavy stress because of your unique biomechanics during exercises, they are likely to hurt when you engage in your sport for a prolonged time. After recovery, if you re-establish your desired training load without modification to your biomechanics, your knees are likely to be injured again.
2. The second predictor of injury is probably the number of consecutive days of training you carry out each week. Scientific studies strongly suggest that reducing the number of consecutive days of training can lower the risk of injury. Recovery time reduces injury rates by giving muscles and connective tissues an opportunity to restore and repair themselves between training.

Psychological factors

Some studies have shown that athletes who are aggressive, tense and compulsive have a higher risk of injury than their relaxed peers. Tension may make muscles and tendons tauter, increasing the risk that they will be harmed during training.

Weak muscles

Many injuries are caused by weak muscles, which simply are not ready to handle the specific demands of your sport. This is why people who start a running programme for the first time often do well for a few weeks but then, as they add the mileage on, suddenly develop foot or ankle problems, hamstring soreness or perhaps lower back pain. Their bodies simply are not strong enough to cope with the demands of the increased training load. For this reason, it is always wise to couple resistance training with regular training.

Muscle imbalance

Screening for muscle imbalances is the current cutting edge of injury prevention. The rationale behind this is that there are detectable and correctable abnormalities of muscle strength and length that are fundamental to the development of almost all musculoskeletal pain and dysfunction. Detection of these abnormalities and correction before injury has occurred should be part of any injury prevention strategy. Assessment of muscle strength and balance and regular sports massage can be beneficial in this strategy.

Muscle stiffness

Muscle stiffness refers to the ratio between the change in muscle resistance and the change in muscle length. Muscle stiffness is thought to be directly related to muscle injury risk so it is important to reduce muscle stiffness as part of a warm-up. Research has indicated that only dynamic stretches, slow controlled movements through the full range of motion, decrease muscle stiffness. Static exercises did not decrease muscle stiffness.

This suggests that dynamic stretches are the most appropriate exercises for warming up and not static stretching exercises. Static stretches are perhaps more appropriate for the warm-down as they help to relax the muscles and increase their range of movement.

Make it specific

Resistance training can fortify muscles and make them less susceptible to damage, especially if the strength-building exercises involve movements that are similar to those associated with the sport. Time should be devoted to developing the muscle groups appropriate to the demands of your sport. If you are a thrower then lots of time should be spent developing muscles at the front of the shoulder. This increases the force with which you can throw, but you must also work systematically on the muscles at the back of the shoulder which control and stabilise the shoulder joint.

Injury prevention tips

- avoid training when you are tired
- increase your consumption of carbohydrate during periods of heavy training
- increases in training should be matched with increases in resting
- any increase in training load should be preceded by an increase in strengthening
- treat even seemingly minor injuries very carefully to prevent them becoming a big problem
- if you experience pain when training, *stop* your training session immediately
- never train hard if you are stiff from the previous effort
- pay attention to hydration and nutrition
- use appropriate training surfaces
- check training and competition areas are clear of hazards
- check equipment is appropriate and safe to use
- introduce new activities very gradually
- allow lots of time for warming up and cooling down
- check over training and competition courses beforehand
- train on different surfaces, using the right footwear
- shower and change immediately after the cool-down
- aim for maximum comfort when travelling
- stay away from infectious areas when training or competing very hard
- be extremely fussy about hygiene in hot weather
- monitor daily for signs of fatigue; if in doubt, ease off
- have regular sports massage.

We'll look at some of these in more detail later on.

Coaches

The key is rapid action when the injury first appears and a lot of psychological support to back up the remedial treatment. Educate yourself and your athletes in the art of cryotherapy (more about this later on). It is when things are not going well that the athlete really needs their coach. It is important for the coach to have an alternative training programme to help the athlete through the injury recovery period.

Brian Mackenzie

Eliminate training errors and reduce your chances of getting hurt

It is well accepted that one major cause of distance running injuries are training errors committed by the athlete concerned. In one study, James and colleagues (1978) were expecting to show that anatomical and biomechanical factors were the most likely causes of running injuries. However, contrary to their hypothesis, they found that some 60% of the injuries in their survey were due to training errors. Other researchers such as Brody (1980) and Clement and colleagues (1981) confirm that training errors are a highly significant, if not the most common, cause of running injury.

If you commit a training error, it does not mean that you are doing the wrong type of training. Instead, training errors are generally associated with high volumes or intensities of training, or any rapid changes in training. This may mean that you are doing the right type of training but just too much of it, or too much training too soon. For example, two common training errors athletes commit are periods of high mileage without easy days in between and sudden major increases in mileage.

Why training errors cause injury becomes obvious when you think about what happens to your body when you train. During a training run the bones, joints and muscles in the legs and low back are stressed and this causes damage. Thus a recovery period must follow the training. During the recovery, the damage is repaired. In time, regular training combined with adequate rest results in what is called 'supercompensation'.

With supercompensation, the body responds to the stress by growing stronger. This happens to all the bones, ligaments, tendons and muscles. Once stronger, the bones and joints can handle greater stress, absorb more shock and the muscles can act more efficiently. However, if you continue with high-mileage training day after day, there is never sufficient recovery. In time, instead of growing stronger, your body becomes permanently weakened and an injury will result.

The same is true if you suddenly increase (>10%) your mileage. Your body is not currently conditioned for the higher levels of stress and so injury results. The bones, ligaments, tendons and muscles are only ever as strong as their current training level. They cannot suddenly develop extra strength as an immediate response to training increases. Supercompensation is a long-term progressive adaptation, not a short-term acute reaction.

Coaches and athletes are well aware that they have to get a positive training effect in muscular strength, anaerobic metabolism and aerobic metabolism. What they too often forget is that positive training effects must also occur in bones, ligaments and tendons if the athlete is to train injury-free.

Avoiding these two common training errors – prolonged high mileage and sudden mileage increases – is a major priority for any athlete. The first step in ironing out these errors is careful planning of training. Athletes must never train on a willy-nilly, do-what-they-feel-like basis. They should always plan every element of their training, including rest days. Then they must ensure that the plan is followed, avoiding extra training just because things happen to be going well.

Many athletes make the mistake of planning their high-quality running sessions, but make up the 'steady runs' element of their training as they go along. This is wrong. For each month, you should plan your training in every detail. Any planned increases in mileage should never be greater than 10% a week. A full rest day is recommended once a week or every other week. Easy days are recommended every three days.

Slow and steady does it

The crucial underlying principle in correct planning is for slow and steady progression. The starting point is to work out what level of mileage you can currently train at without becoming injured. Then you must plan a slow progression over a period of months up to the mileage level you would like to be training at. As well as being the correct practice for injury prevention, this long, slow progression of training is also the key to improved performance. Common sense says that an athlete who attempts an 80-miles-a-week regime but regularly takes weeks off through injury will not be as fit as the athlete who starts on 40 miles a week, slowly builds up 60 and continues injury-free.

Prolonged high mileage and sudden increases in mileage are not the only kinds of training errors. In fact, just about any rapid change in any aspect of training could be classed as a training error and likely to cause injury.

A sudden addition of high-intensity training is another common training error. This could be the situation when, say, you have spent months on steady mileage training and then decide to include fast anaerobic interval sessions. The same principle applies. The body has not yet been trained to cope with running at a fast pace, with the higher muscle forces and impact forces that result from increased speed. The muscles tire quickly so extra strain is placed on the bones and joints. The result is injury.

Again, slow and planned progressions are the way to avoid this training error. A good way to start with higher-intensity sessions is with a fartlek workout once a week (this involves including fast sessions in your run when you feel like it, taking easy sections for recovery). After a few weeks of fartlek runs you can then add an interval session at 3k pace. For example, start with an eight to 10 x 400m with 60 seconds' recovery, building up to 25 x 400m. Once you can cope with this pace, you can attempt faster-paced sessions to train the anaerobic system.

Another example of a training error is a sudden change in running surface. Hard surfaces, such as roads, require high-impact forces to be absorbed. Obviously you must be able to cope with this. However, at the same time hard surfaces are true and do not dampen the propulsive forces. Conversely, soft off-road terrains attenuate impact forces, thus lessening the need to absorb shock, but dampen the propulsive forces. This means you may have to change your neuromuscular coordination to adapt.

If you train regularly on hard surfaces and then switch to training on soft surfaces, or you do a one-off cross-country race, problems may occur due to the different stress on the muscles. If you regularly train on soft terrain and then switch to hard surfaces, you will suffer because you cannot cope with the high impact forces.

Artificial surfaces also have unique properties that you must be used to coping with. If athletes are to train or race on different surfaces, they must plan in advance the switch in surface and build up the training on the new surface slowly.

Compounding the problem

The worst kinds of training errors are compound rapid changes. The classic compound change that runners make is to spend all winter doing steady running on the road in trainers and then switch to fast training on the track, in spikes, for the summer season. Here there are three variables that have suddenly been changed: the intensity of the running sessions, the surface and the shoe. With spikes there is lower heel lift and less support. This means there is greater dorsiflexion and potentially more pronation. This will place greater stress on the muscles in the lower leg.

This change in biomechanics caused by the shoes, along with the higher impact forces from the fast speeds and different muscle recruitment required for the spongy nature of the track, is often too much for the athlete and injury will result. However, if you include some speed training on the track, in spikes, throughout the whole training year, you will dramatically reduce injury risks in the spring when you want to increase intensities for track racing. As long as you are used to, and can cope with, a variety of surfaces or shoes, that is fine. Remember, it is rapid changes that have to be eliminated, not necessarily variety.

The training errors I have mentioned are typical of those committed by distance runners – but not just by them. Coaches and athletes of all events and sports must realise that prolonged high-intensity training, prolonged high volumes of training or any kind of rapid change in any aspect of training should be seen as a training error. This is a vital principle to understand. It should be followed in any training programme or potential improvement will only be curtailed by injury.

Clearly, then, it is very important for injury prevention to avoid training errors.

With careful planning and slow progressions, athletes should be able to avoid the kinds of errors I have discussed.

But a word of warning: because elite performance requires high mileage and high-intensity training, athletes are still at risk simply from hard training. Some may be able to withstand it while others may need to reduce their training to remain injury-free. Only then will they reap the benefits of uninterrupted training. To underline the point, here is a telling comment from Derek Clayton, the former world-class marathon runner:

'If I had my competitive career to run over again, I would change some of my attitudes to injuries. I would show them more respect. Because, after all, injuries were not some unknown barrier I was trying to break through. Injuries were simply my body telling me that something wrong was happening.'

References

Brody, DM (1980), 'Running Injuries', *Clin Symp*, 32(4), pp1-36

Clement, DB, Taunton, JE, Smart, GW, and Nicol, KL (1981), 'A survey of overuse running injuries', *Phy Sp Med*, 9(5), pp47-58

James, SL, Bates, BT, and Osternig, LR (1978), 'Injuries to runners: A study of entrants to a 10K race', *Am J Sp Med*, 6, pp40-50

Taunton, JE (1993), 'Training errors', in *Sports Injuries: Basic Principles of prevention and care.* in Renstrom PAFH (Ed), London: Blackwell

Raphael Brandon

Why detecting muscle imbalance is an essential part of an injury prevention strategy

Screening athletes prior to competition and training is increasingly being undertaken as part of a comprehensive injury prevention strategy. Coaches, trainers and athletes need to have a working understanding of risk management strategies to reduce injury risk. Clearly not all injuries are preventable. Rugby footballers will sustain impact injuries no matter how well conditioned and protected they are, but the risk of injury can be minimised.

Injuries can be classified in many ways but perhaps the most helpful classification divides them into acute and overuse types. Acute injuries happen suddenly and may be direct (resulting from collisions with opponents, the ground or playing equipment) or indirect (for example, sudden muscle pulls). Overuse injuries result from repetitive micro-damage to the body from sporting activity that exceeds the body's ability to repair such damage (stress fractures, Achilles tendinosis, 'shin splints' etc).

Acute indirect and overuse injuries are theoretically preventable. By reducing the risk of sustaining such injuries we will be able to maximise the ability to sustain a training load, reduce time out of competition and training and hence enhance performance.

Injury prevention strategies

These in the main are well known and include:
- an adequate warm-up and cool-down
- appropriate training loads
- appropriate surfaces to train on
- the use of person-specific equipment (matching running shoes to foot type, appropriately set-up bicycles etc)
- adequate recovery times
- attention to hydration and nutrition.

Pre-participation screening is increasingly being added to the above list, especially in the elite sport arena.

Pre-participation screening

This is commonplace in the USA, where in excess of 6 million adolescent athletes each year are screened to detect any condition that may limit participation or may predispose to injury. The impetus for these programmes is provided by the need for colleges and high schools to meet insurance or legal requirements. Such screening principally looks for conditions that would disqualify an athlete from competition and consequently the focus is on recognising undiagnosed and serious medical problems.

Heart conditions such as hypertrophic obstructive cardiomyopathy and aortic stenosis are specifically looked for in athletes with a history of dizziness or faintness during exercise. Marfans syndrome, a disorder of connective tissue that may lead to a rupture of the thoracic aorta and sudden death during exercise, is typically only seen in tall athletes and basketballers are specifically screened for this condition.

The musculoskeletal element of the screening typically focuses on specific joints such as the knee, ankle and shoulder and aims to detect current injury and deficits resulting from previous injury. The focus of these examinations is the joint itself rather than the surrounding muscles and the examiner assesses the range of joint movement, the presence of excess fluid in the joint and the integrity of the supporting ligaments. Such screening does not usually specifically look for muscle imbalance.

Muscle imbalance screening

Screening for muscle imbalances is the current cutting edge of pre-participation screening. The rationale behind such an approach is that there are detectable and correctable abnormalities of muscle strength and length that are fundamental to the development of almost all musculoskeletal pain and dysfunction. Detection of these abnormalities and correction before injury has occurred should be part of any injury prevention strategy and a similar approach will ensure that injuries, once sustained, will not recur.

Muscle imbalance – basic principles

The relationship between the tone or strength and length of the muscles around a joint is known as muscle balance. When examining an athlete we need to assess stationary and dynamic strength and length. Muscles can be divided into two types, mobilisers and stabilisers. These two groups of muscles have quite different characteristics. The mobilisers are found close to the body's surface and tend to cross two joints. They are typically made up of fast-twitch fibres that produce power but lack endurance. With time and use they tend to tighten and shorten. Stabilisers, by contrast, are situated deeper, invariably only cross one joint and are made up of slow-twitch fibres for endurance. They tend to become weak and long with time.

Functionally the stabilisers assist postural holding and work against gravity. The mobilisers assist rapid or ballistic movement and produce high force. While initially both groups of muscles work in a complementary fashion to stabilise and move, over time the mobilisers can inhibit the action of the stabilisers and begin to move and attempt to stabilise on their own. This inhibition of the stabilisers and preferential recruitment of the mobilisers is central to the development of 'imbalance' and is the essence of what we want to detect and if possible reverse.

Typical imbalance patterns

Groin injuries are the bane of athletes and therapists alike. Accounting for 5% of all sports injuries, they are often of the overuse type and typically the athlete will have had pain for a considerable period of time. The 'holy trinity' of chronic groin injuries are the sports hernia (disruption to the inguinal canal without an apparent hernia), osteitis pubis (inflammation or degeneration of the pubic symphysis) and chronic adductor tendinosis (degeneration or wear at the origin of the adductor tendons of the inner thigh). Athletes may develop one, two or all three of the above. All of these conditions are thought to be caused by repetitive shearing forces acting across the pubic symphysis (the joint at the front of the pelvis where the two pubic bones meet). What the unfortunate sufferers often have in common is poor pelvic stability where they are unable to stabilise the lower abdomen and pelvis while performing the twisting and turning movements needed for their sport. When this group is examined for muscle imbalances we invariably find that their mobilisers, the hamstrings, adductors, hip flexors and abdominal recti, have become shortened and their principal stabilisers, the transversus abdominis and posterior glutei mediae, have become long, weak and inhibited. The mobilisers are attempting to stabilise as well as mobilise and perform neither role particularly well.

Similar imbalances in the shoulder are seen in overhead athletes where the stabilising group of muscles, principally the lower trapezius and serratus anterior (which stabilise the scapula or shoulder blade) are long and weak, the rotator cuff is weak and as a consequence we find increased translation or movement at the glenohumeral joint leading to pain and dysfunction.

Screening

Assessing muscle length is not overly difficult as there are standard tests. Assessing strength is more taxing. One needs the athlete (and assessor) to be able to isolate the action of individual muscles. Most strength testing to date has concentrated on mobilisers rather than stabilisers because the former are easier to isolate. The assessor needs to develop a protocol whereby both groups are assessed. This is carried out statically and dynamically.

Injury prevention

This process is typified by three elements that run concurrently. One lengthens the shortened mobilisers at the same time as training the stabilisers to work again, initially statically and then dynamically. In the groin this would typically involve shortening and stabilising the transversus abdominis, multifidus and gluteals and lengthening the tensor fascia latae/Iliotibial band (TFL/ITB), rectus femoris, psoas and invariably the hamstrings.

Dr Simon Kemp and Chris Boynes

Ten practical guidelines that will help an athlete avoid getting injured

A man's greatest strength is often his greatest weakness and this is particularly noticeable among full-time sportsmen and women. The compulsive streak in their character, which drives them to practise hour after hour, day after day, is their worst enemy when it comes to handling injuries. The only way around this is to put 'avoidance of injury' high on the list of priorities. When I am making out a training plan I always start with the objectives such things as improving aerobic fitness, practising changes of pace or maintaining flexibility. Including 'avoidance of injury' in this list brings it into the reckoning when planning a week's training. These are my guidelines, some of which we've already briefly touched upon:
1. never train hard when stiff from the previous effort
2. introduce new activities very gradually

3. allow lots of time for warming up and cooling down
4. check over training and competition courses beforehand
5. train on different surfaces, using the right footwear
6. shower and change immediately after the cool-down
7. aim for the maximum comfort when travelling
8. stay away from infectious areas when training or competing very hard
9. be extremely fussy about hygiene in hot weather
10. monitor the athlete daily for signs of fatigue. If in doubt, ease off.

Never train hard when stiff

This seems obvious but it is seen all too often at the beginning of a season or in a training camp. Some people turn up very fit and set a fast pace in training and the others suffer for it the next day. But instead of waiting for the stiffness to go, they try to go on training as hard as the day before. The result is that running is awkward, movements are not coordinated and injuries are more likely.

Introduce new activities gradually

Ideally, one would never introduce anything new at all, but there has to be a first time for everything and there are bound to be changes of emphasis, *eg* the switch from indoor to outdoor training or from grass to a synthetic surface. The solution is to start switching well before it is necessary. In switching from cross-country running to the synthetic track, for example, one might include a bit of running on the track whenever the opportunity arises, even if it is only three or four laps and a few strides. The first track session of the year would only be half a normal session and it would be done mostly in trainers. The following week one might do most of one session on the track but only part of it in spikes, and for the next two weeks one increases the proportion done in spikes. After a month, we might be running three times a week on the track, with other sessions being done mostly on grass.

Warming up and cooling down

In the British climate this is particularly necessary. Warm muscles stretch much better than cold muscles. Ligaments and tendons are much more likely to tear when the muscles are cold and inflexible.

The warm-up procedure helps in several other ways, too, both physically in diverting the blood flow from non-essential areas to working muscles, and mentally, in focusing the athlete on the approaching event.

I would recommend at least 15 minutes and up to 30 minutes of warm-up before hard training starts. In ball games this can often be done with a ball, carrying out various skill routines, but in all cases it should start with five to 10 minutes of gentle movement, gradually increasing in pace, followed by five to 10 minutes of stretching, still in warm clothing. After that, one moves to fast strides and eventually to short sprints, then stays warm and loose until the start. A sprinter might well take 45 minutes to warm up for a 10-second burst of energy. During the cool-down period, which should last for 10 to 15 minutes after a competition or a hard training session, the body temperature returns to normal and the fatigue products are flushed out of the muscles, which reduces the chances of stiffness the next day.

Check the course beforehand

In cross-country and road running there may be unexpected traps for the unwary, potholes in the road, sudden ups or downs, all of which could cause trouble if you are not prepared for them, and of course this is closely linked to the next rule.

Wear the right shoes

Wearing shoes which are too light or flimsy or which are unevenly worn are two very common causes of injury. If you turn up expecting a soft course and find that it is frozen hard, you could be in a lot of trouble. I once arrived for a so-called cross-country race in Madrid to find that it was 90% road. Luckily I had brought my road racing shoes, but my colleague, who had only spikes, had to run the race in dance shoes strapped on with pink ribbon! (I won, but he came second.) At a higher level, Liz McColgan threw away a chance of winning the world cross-country title in Boston because she had not checked out the length of spikes necessary on the snow-covered course.

Perhaps the commonest cause of all injuries is training too much on hard surfaces. Running fast on roads causes a lot of impact shock. I recommend getting off the road at least one day in three.

Shower and change after training

This reduces the likelihood of stiffening up and your chances of catching a cold. Ideally, a hard session or a race should always be followed by a massage if you want to recover quickly.

Travel in comfort

This sounds a bit sissy, but it is not at all uncommon for athletes to stay wedged into a minibus or a train, sitting awkwardly for several hours before an important event. I recommend that you get up, walk around and stretch once every hour while travelling, if possible. Apart from the muscles, the more you can keep down the stress, the better you will perform. It is best to get to the venue the day before the event for anything big, and if you have to deal with major changes in climate and/or time zones it is best to get there a week beforehand.

Avoid infection

After hard sessions, the immune system is definitely vulnerable. Athletes in hard training are particularly susceptible before a big event. They should stay away from crowded rooms, schools and people with bad colds.

Be fussy about hygiene

All too often people in training camps or in games villages pick up stomach bugs just before the big event and the reason is often evident from the sloppy conditions in which they live, with food left around, dirty clothing, people sharing cups and glasses. Athletes, like most young people, have a sense of invulnerability, which is positively dangerous.

Monitor fatigue

In hindsight it is usually possible to trace the cause of an illness or injury, and there is usually a point where the athletes should have eased off but did not. It is a vital part of the coach's job to tell the athlete when to stop and the athlete must play their part by being aware of the early signs of overtiredness. A raised resting pulse is a sure sign.

Attitude to injury

However careful you are, injuries can occur, particularly in the stress of competition and illness can be picked up, often when the athlete is really fit.

The first thing is damage limitation. The usual course of events is as follows:
1. The athlete feels a little pain during training and ignores it.
2. The pain recurs, and may even be felt after training, but is not bad enough to prevent training.
3. The pain is now bad enough to interfere with normal training, but the athlete can still compete, if they rest.
4. The pain is so bad that the athlete can neither train nor compete.

The time to report the injury and start treatment is at stage one. The procedure should be to switch right away from any exercise that makes the injury more painful and to get diagnosis immediately, certainly not later than the next day. At the same time, coach and athlete should work out what forms of exercise are possible, and redesign the programme so that the athlete is at least doing something to maintain cardiovascular fitness, constant body weight and muscle strength. It is as important to maintain their morale and confidence as it is to maintain their fitness, but in these days of leisure centres, gyms, static bikes and aqua joggers it is always possible to find some suitable exercise.

To take an example:

I had a case where a runner was tripped and fell, tearing some fibres just below the kneecap, three weeks before the Olympic trials. After icing it (more about cryotherapy in a moment) and protecting it for the first two days, he started on daily physiotherapy and massaged the area before each session to stimulate blood flow. He could not cycle with it but he could walk, do some circuit training and swim front crawl. After three days of this he progressed to walking and jogging on grass, then to long uphill jogs, trying to avoid limping. Running uphill on grass means there is very little stress but the heart is working quite hard. By the 10th day he was doing long slow training; by the 14th day he was able to train hard, but still mainly uphill on grass. In the third week he was able to do part of the session on the track and at the end of the week he went into the trials with no knee problem at all and finished second, qualifying for the Olympic team.

The key is rapid action when the injury first appears and a lot of psychological support to back up the remedial treatment. It is when things are not going well that the athlete really needs their coach.

Bruce Tulloh

Cryotherapy to the rescue

Cryotherapy is the use of cooling as a means of treating injuries, and may be used in different ways on both acute and chronic injuries. Much research has been carried out on the effects of cooling on damaged soft tissues, and although the benefits are now widely accepted there are varying opinions on how long the application should be to gain maximum benefit. Meanwhile there are still many athletes who believe a long soak in a hot bath after an injury is the best remedy to ease the pain.

The body's reaction to an injury

In many instances, no matter how small the injury, tissues will either have been stretched or have received an impact causing blood vessels to be torn or damaged. The extent of bleeding will depend on the vascularity of the tissues involved, and may also be increased if the injury occurs during exercise. Blood will flow out until the vessels are restricted (vasoconstriction), so preventing further blood leaking into the tissues. It is important to stop bleeding into tissues as the blood will act as an irritant, increase inflammation and must be cleared from the tissues before the healing process can properly commence.

Cells starved of nourishment from the blood due to injury will soon die. These dying cells stimulate the release of histamine, causing the blood vessels to dilate and thereby bringing increased blood supply and extra nutrients to help repair and rebuild the damaged tissues. During this phase of increased but slower and more viscous blood supply, the capillary walls become much more permeable and quantities of protein and inflammatory substances are pushed into the area, causing swelling. Various reactions continue at a rapid rate, all of which contribute to the healing process.

Muscle spasm may also occur, causing the muscle to contract either voluntarily or involuntarily, helping prevent further movement. However, this may have adverse effects by further restricting blood flow and also placing more pressure on nerve endings, leading to increased pain.

RICE

By applying ice or cooling immediately after an injury involving damage to soft tissues, the level of swelling and amount of blood allowed to leak out may be substantially limited. This will also be assisted by compression, elevation and rest, hence 'ICER' – or more commonly 'RICE'.

Ice – Apply ice for up to 10 minutes as soon after the injury as possible, do not wait for the swelling to start. This may be repeated every two hours during the first two days after injury. It is important not to keep the ice on any longer than 10 minutes as the body then reacts by increasing blood flow to warm the area and therefore exacerbating the swelling. Do not apply ice directly to the skin. Use a wet flannel.

Compression – After ice, apply a compression bandage to help minimise the swelling to the tissues.

Elevation – Elevate the injured part to help limit blood flow and prevent use of muscles to injured part.

Rest the injured part as much as possible to allow the healing of damaged tissues.

Failure to do this means that the period of recovery from injury may be considerably extended while the swelling and removal of dead tissue and blood cells is dealt with. If severe and not properly managed, these may create long-term problems for the athlete.

Use of ice

When applying ice, never do so directly onto the skin as this may result in ice burns to the skin. Wrap the ice in a damp cloth (a dry cloth will not transmit cold effectively). There is an on-going debate over how long to apply ice, and current research suggests that during the acute phase (*ie* the first 24 to 48 hours after injury), 10 minutes is the maximum time needed and may be adjusted downwards according to the depth of tissues it is being applied to. Application for the appropriate time must be repeated every two hours during the acute phase. Once only after injury is not enough!

If the ice pack is left on for more than 10 minutes, a reflex reaction occurs (hunting effect) where the blood vessels dilate and blood is again pumped into the injured area, causing further bleeding and swelling.

Ice will have an analgesic effect on the injured part by limiting the pain and swelling; muscle spasm may also be reduced. While this has obvious benefits, be cautious about reducing the pain, as this may also mask the seriousness of the injury.

After an initial healing period of up to 72 hours (depending on the severity of the injury), ice massage may be incorporated into treatments. By applying stroking movements with an ice pack, the blood vessels will dilate and constrict alternately, bringing an increased supply of blood and nutrients to the area and so increasing the rate of healing. This may be done for more than 10 minutes to increase circulation.

Contra-indications of using ice

- Check a person's general sensitivity to ice. Some people find the application of cold immediately painful.
- Do not use ice on injuries in the chest region as in some instances this may cause a reaction in the muscles, bringing about angina pain, possibly from the constriction of coronary arteries.
- Always check skin sensitivity before applying ice. If a person cannot feel touch before applying ice, this may indicate other problems such as nerve impingement. In such instances ice would only serve to mask this and complicate the problem.
- Do not apply cold to someone with high blood pressure as vasoconstriction will increase the pressure within the vessels.

Education

It is important to educate anyone managing injuries, including athletes themselves, on at least the basic use of ice on soft tissue injuries. Early treatment is essential.

Brian Mackenzie

Mobility

Introduction

Physical fitness is more than just endurance or muscular strength. It is a complex latticework of many interrelated factors, each important in its own way. One of these factors is flexibility – perhaps the most neglected aspect of many fitness programmes. Flexibility training is being increasingly recognised as crucial for complementing muscular strength, building efficiency and coordination and preventing injuries.

Flexibility, mobility and suppleness all mean the range of limb movement around joints. Mobility is the ability to perform a joint action through a range of movement. In any movement there are two groups of muscles at work:
- protagonistic muscles which cause the movement to take place
- antagonistic muscles which oppose the movement and determine the amount of mobility.

Mobility plays an important part in the preparation of athletes by developing a range of movement to allow technical development and assisting in the prevention of injury.

Overview of the mobility module

In this module Brian Mackenzie looks at how you can develop your flexibility and mobility, with articles providing:
- an overview of the types of stretching
- exercise for the upper body
- exercises and drills targeted at conditioning the legs
- examples of dynamic stretching and mobility exercises, which could form part of the warm-up programme in a training session

- examples of static stretching and mobility exercises which could form part of the cool-down programme at the end of a training session.

The articles in this module are applicable to most sports.

What types of stretching are there?

The various techniques of stretching may be grouped as static, ballistic and assisted. In both static and ballistic exercises the athlete is in control of the movements. In assisted, the movement is controlled by an external force which is usually a partner.

Static stretching

Static stretching involves gradually easing into the stretch position and holding the position. The amount of time a static stretch is held may be anything from six seconds to two minutes. Often in static stretching you are advised to move further into the stretch position as the stretch sensation subsides.

Dynamic or ballistic stretching

Ballistic stretching involves some form of rapid movement into the required stretch position. Where the event requires a ballistic movement, then it is appropriate and perhaps necessary to conduct ballistic stretching exercises. Start off with the movement at half speed for a couple of repetitions and then gradually work up to full speed.

Assisted stretching

Assisted stretching involves the assistance of a partner who must fully understand what their role is – otherwise the risk of injury is high. A partner can be employed to assist with partner stretches and proprioceptive neuromuscular facilitation (PNF) techniques.

Partner stretching

Your partner helps you to maintain the stretch position or to ease into the stretch position as the sensation of stretch subsides. You should aim to be fully relaxed and breathe easily throughout the exercise. Partner-assisted stretches are best used as developmental exercises, with each stretch being held for 30 seconds.

PNF technique

1. Move into the stretch position so that you feel the stretch sensation.
2. Your partner holds the limb in this stretched position.
3. You then push against your partner by contracting the antagonistic muscles for six to 10 seconds and then relax. During the contraction your partner aims to resist any movement of the limb.
4. Your partner then moves the limb further into the stretch until you feel the stretch sensation.
5. Go back to step 2 (Repeat this procedure three or four times before the stretch is released).

Which method is best?

Static methods produce far fewer instances of muscle soreness, injury and damage to connective tissues than ballistic methods. Static methods are simple to carry out and may be conducted virtually anywhere. For maximum gains in flexibility in the shortest possible time, PNF technique is the most appropriate. Dynamic (ballistic), slowed controlled movements through the full range of the motion will reduce muscle stiffness. Where the technique requires ballistic movement, ballistic stretches should be employed.

In what order should you use the mobility methods?

When conducting mobility exercises it is recommended to perform them in the following order: static, assisted and then dynamic.

When should they be performed?

Mobility exercises could be part of:
- the warm-up programme
- a stand-alone unit of work.

It is considered beneficial to conduct mobility exercises as part of the cool-down programme but this should not include ballistic exercises as the muscles are fatigued and more prone to injury. Static exercises are recommended as they relax the muscles and increase their range of movement.

Brian Mackenzie

Upper body conditioning

One of the most common sites of injury is the lower back. Injury in this region can be as a result of muscular imbalance, weak or inflexible muscles or poor posture. It makes sense, therefore, to identify a session that will work all these areas and develop the right level of conditioning for injury prevention.

The exercises

Detailed below is a session of eight exercises. The exercises are to be performed *slowly* and *smoothly* and at no time should you be out of breath.

Sit-ups (upper abdominals)

- lie on your back with your legs bent, knees together and feet flat on the floor
- rest your hands on your thighs
- sit up until the palms of your hands touch your knees
- return to the starting position
- perform the movements in a slow, controlled fashion.

Back arches (back)

- lie on your front with your legs crossed at the ankles, keeping your feet firmly anchored to the floor
- keep your hands and arms straight out in front of you
- raise your upper body off the floor, keeping your neck in line with your spine
- hold for one second and then slowly lower to the floor.

Reverse curl (lower abdominals)

- lie on your back with your legs bent, knees together and feet flat on the floor
- curl up your legs and buttocks off the floor
- return to the starting position
- perform the movements in a slow controlled fashion.

Hip and leg raise (gluteals and hamstrings)

- lie on your back with knees bent, feet flat on the floor
- place your hands by your side
- raise hips and straighten one leg, then hold for a second before lowering
- repeat with the other leg.

Transversus abdominis (abdominal)

- place yourself in the kneeling position with your hands on the ground
- hips directly above the knees

- shoulders directly above the hands
- keep the spine in a natural position
- relax the abdominal muscles and let the tummy sag down
- gently pull your tummy button and the area below it towards your spine
- hold for 10 to 15 seconds and then relax.

Short sit-ups (hip flexors and abdominals)

- lie on your back with knees bent, feet flat on the floor
- rest your hands lightly on the side of your head (not the back of your neck)
- raise your body so that your upper body is at a 30 to 40-degree angle with the floor
- hold for one second before coming down slowly.

Back extensions (back)

- sit on the floor with legs bent, feet flat on the floor
- position your hands on the floor behind you to take some of the weight
- raise your body off the floor so that your body is parallel with the floor
- hold for one second and slowly lower.

Twisted curl (oblique abdominals)

- lie on your back with your legs bent, knees together and feet flat on the floor
- place the left ankle on the right knee with the left knee pointing away
- curl the right shoulder up to the left knee
- keep lower back on the ground
- return to the starting position
- perform the movements in a slow controlled fashion
- repeat with the other leg and shoulder.

How many and how often?

Start at one set of 10 repetitions. Each week increase the number of repetitions by two. When you reach 20 repetitions increase the number of sets by one and start again at 10 repetitions. The exercises should be performed two or three times a week and be incorporated into your training schedule.

Before you start

Prior to starting any training programme, it is recommend that you have a medical examination to ensure that it is safe for you to do so.

Brian Mackenzie

Leg conditioning

Introduction

This section of the Mobility module identifies general and specific exercise programmes to develop the legs. To gain any real benefit it requires at least 16 weeks of continuous exercise.

General drills

The following drills should be performed over 20 to 30m. Start with two sets and increment in steps of 10m per two weeks. When you get to 30m add an extra set and start again at 20m. Perform the drill, jog for 20m and walk back – five minutes' recovery per set.
- walk on toes
- walk on heels
- bum kicks with high knee
- skip with high knees
- jog with high knees
- skips for height
- side strides.

Specific drills

The following plyometric drills should be performed six to 10 times. Start with two sets and increment in steps of two repetitions per week. When you get to 10 repetitions add an extra set and start again at six repetitions. Perform the drill, jog for 20m and walk back – five minutes' recovery per set.
- bounds
- bunny hops for distance
- bunny hops with high knee for height
- single leg hop with high knee.

Specific exercises

The following exercises should be performed for 30 to 60 seconds. Start with two sets and increment in 10-second steps. When you get to 60 seconds, add an extra set and start again at 30 seconds – 30 seconds' recovery between each exercise and five minutes per set:
- single leg squat
- legs forward astride squat
- single leg squat hops
- legs forward astride jump squat - swapping leg positions
- skipping or bounce on toes
- running step-ups onto a bench
- astride jumps onto a bench
- sideways hopping over six-inch hurdle.

Multi-gym exercise

The following exercises should be performed using weights of 60% of your maximum for the exercise – alternate with an upper body exercise. Start at two sets of 10 repetitions, increment by two repetitions each week. When you get to 16 repetitions, add an extra set and start again at 10 repetitions – 30 seconds' recovery per rep and five minutes' recovery per set:

- standing heel raise
- sitting hamstring curls
- sitting leg press
- lying reverse hamstring curls
- half squats
- step-ups.

Brian Mackenzie

Dynamic stretching exercises

Overview

The following are examples of dynamic stretching and mobility exercises, which could form part of the warm-up programme in a training session. The dynamic exercises you incorporate into your warm-up programme should be appropriate to the movements you would experience in your sport/event. In all the exercises breathe easily while performing them.

Current research work detailed in *Medicine & Science in Sport and Exercise* 33(3), pp354-358, and *Journal of Strength and Conditioning Research*, vol 15 (1), pp98-101, suggests that the use of dynamic stretches – slow controlled movements through the full range of motion – are the most appropriate exercises for the warm-up. By contrast, static stretches are more appropriate for the cool-down.

The exercises

Joint rotations

From a standing position with your arms hanging loosely at your sides, flex, extend, and rotate each of the following joints:

- fingers
- wrist
- elbows
- shoulders
- neck
- trunk and shoulder blades
- hips
- knees

- ankles
- feet and toes.

Neck mobility

- flexion/extension: tuck your chin into your chest, and then lift your chin upward as far as possible – six to 10 repetitions
- lateral flexion: lower your left ear towards your left shoulder and then your right ear to your right shoulder – six to 10 repetitions
- rotation: turn your chin laterally towards your left shoulder and then rotate it towards your right shoulder – six to 10 repetitions.

Shoulder circles

- stand tall, feet slightly wider than shoulder-width apart, knees slightly bent
- raise your right shoulder towards your right ear, take it backwards, down and then up again to the ear in a smooth action
- repeat with the other shoulder.

Arm swings

- stand tall, feet slightly wider than shoulder-width apart, knees slightly bent
- keep the back straight at all times
- overhead/down and back: swing both arms continuously to an overhead position and then forward, down, and backwards – six to 10 repetitions
- side/front crossover: swing both arms out to your sides and then cross them in front of your chest – six to 10 repetitions.

Side bends

- stand tall with good posture, feet slightly wider than shoulder-width apart, knees slightly bent, hands resting on hips
- lift your trunk up and away from your hips and bend smoothly first to one side, then the other, avoiding the tendency to lean either forwards or backwards
- repeat the whole sequence 16 times with a slow rhythm, breathing out as you bend to the side, and in as you return to the centre.

Hip circles and twists

- circles – with your hands on your hips and feet spread wider than your shoulders, make circles with your hips in a clockwise direction for 10 to 12 repetitions; then repeat in a counter-clockwise direction
- twists – extend your arms out to your sides and twist your torso and hips to the left, shifting your weight on to the left foot; then twist your torso to the right while shifting your weight to the right foot – 10 to 12 repetitions on each side.

Half-squat

- stand tall with good posture, holding your hands out in front of you for balance
- now bend at the knees until your thighs are parallel with the floor
- keep your back long throughout the movement and look straight ahead
- make sure that your knees always point in the same direction as your toes
- once at your lowest point, fully straighten your legs to return to your starting position
- repeat the exercise 16 times with a smooth, controlled rhythm
- breathe in as you descend, and out as you rise.

Leg swings

- **flexion/extension** – stand sideways-on to the wall
- weight on your left leg and your right hand on the wall for balance
- swing your right leg forward and backward
- 10 to 12 repetitions on each leg
- **Cross-body flexion/abduction** – leaning slightly forward with both hands on a wall and your weight on your left leg, swing your right leg to the left in front of your body, pointing your toes upwards as your foot reaches its furthest point of motion
- then swing the right leg back to the right as far as is comfortable, again pointing your toes up as your foot reaches its final point of movement
- 10 to 12 repetitions on each leg.

Lunges

- stand tall with both feet together (starting position)
- keeping the back straight, lunge forward with the right leg approximately 100 to 150cm
- the right thigh should be parallel with the ground and the right lower leg vertical
- spring back to the starting position
- repeat with the left leg
- 12 to 16 repetitions on each leg.

Ankle bounce

- **double leg bounce** – leaning forward with your hands on the wall and your weight on your toes, raise and lower both heels rapidly (bounce)
- each time, lift your heels one to two inches from the ground while maintaining ground contact with the ball of your feet
- 12 to 16 repetitions
- **single leg bounce** – leaning forward with your hands on a wall and all your weight on your left foot, raise the right knee forward while pushing the left heel towards the ground

- then lower the right foot to the floor while raising the left heel one or two inches
- repeat in a rapid, bouncy fashion
- 12 to 16 repetitions on each leg.

Brian Mackenzie

Static stretching exercises

Overview

The following are examples of general static stretching and mobility exercises that could form part of the cool-down programme at the end of a training session. The aim is to relax the muscles and facilitate an improvement in maximum range of motion. In all exercises, breathe easily while performing them and hold the static stretches for 20 seconds.

The exercises

Chest stretch

- stand tall, feet slightly wider than shoulder-width apart, knees slightly bent
- hold your arms out to the side, parallel with the ground, with the palms of the hand facing forward
- stretch the arms back as far as possible
- you should feel the stretch across your chest.

Biceps stretch

- stand tall, feet slightly wider than shoulder-width apart, knees slightly bent
- hold your arms out to the side, parallel with the ground, with the palms of the hands facing forward
- rotate the hands so the palms face to the rear
- stretch the arms back as far as possible
- you should feel the stretch across your chest and in the biceps.

Upper back stretch

- stand tall, feet slightly wider than shoulder-width apart, knees slightly bent
- interlock your fingers and push your hands as far away from your chest as possible, allowing your upper back to relax
- you should feel the stretch between your shoulder blades.

Shoulder stretch

- stand tall, feet slightly wider than shoulder-width apart, knees slightly bent
- place your right arm across the front of your chest, parallel with the ground
- bend the left arm up and use the left forearm to ease the right arm closer to your chest
- you will feel the stretch in the shoulder
- repeat with the other arm.

Shoulder and triceps stretch

- stand tall, feet slightly wider than shoulder-width apart, knees slightly bent
- place both hands above your head and then slide both of your hands down the middle of your spine
- you will feel the stretch in the shoulders and the triceps.

Side bends

- stand tall, feet slightly wider than shoulder-width apart, knees slightly bent, hands resting on the hips
- bend slowly to one side, come back to the vertical position and then bend to the other side
- do not lean forwards or backwards.

Abdominal and lower back muscles

- lie face down on the ground in a prone position
- lift your body off the ground so that you are supported only by your forearms and toes; the elbows should be on the ground and almost directly below your shoulders; your forearms and hands should be resting on the ground, pointed straight ahead; toes and feet should be shoulder-width apart and your head in line with your spine
- contract your gluteus (bum) muscles gently – hold for 10 seconds
- lift your right arm off the ground, straighten it and point it straight ahead, holding it in the air for 10 seconds
- return to the starting position
- repeat with the left arm
- return to starting position
- lift your right leg off the ground and hold it there for 10 seconds (keep back straight)
- return to starting position
- repeat with left leg
- return to starting position
- lift your right arm and left leg simultaneously and hold them in position for 10 seconds
- return to starting position

- lift your left arm and right leg simultaneously and hold them in position for 10 seconds
- return to the starting position.

Hamstring stretch

- sit on the ground with both legs straight out in front of you
- bend the left leg and place the sole of the left foot alongside the knee of the right leg
- allow the left leg to lie relaxed on the ground
- bend forward, keeping the back straight
- you will feel the stretch in the hamstring of the right leg
- repeat with the other leg.

Calf stretch

- stand tall with one leg in front of the other, hands flat and at shoulder height against a wall
- ease your back leg further away from the wall, keeping it straight and press the heel firmly into the floor
- keep your hips facing the wall and the rear leg and spine in a straight line
- you will feel the stretch in the calf of the rear leg
- repeat with the other leg.

Hip and thigh stretch

- stand tall with your feet approximately two shoulder-widths apart
- turn the feet and face to the right
- bend the right leg so that the right thigh is parallel with the ground and the right lower leg is vertical
- gradually lower the body
- keep your back straight and use the arms to balance
- you will feel the stretch along the front of the left thigh and along the hamstrings of the right leg
- repeat by turning and facing to the left.

Adductor stretch

- stand tall with your feet approximately two shoulder-widths apart
- bend the right leg and lower the body
- keep your back straight and use the arms to balance
- you will feel the stretch in the left leg adductor
- repeat with the left leg.

Groin stretch

- sit with tall posture
- ease both of your feet up towards your body and place the soles of your feet together, allowing your knees to come up and out to the side
- resting your hands on your lower legs or ankles, ease both knees towards the ground
- you will feel the stretch along the inside of your thighs and groin.

Front of trunk stretch

- lie face down on the floor, fully outstretched
- bring your hands to the sides of your shoulders and ease your chest off the floor, keeping your hips firmly pressed into the ground
- you will feel the stretch in the front of the trunk.

Iliotibial band stretch

- sit tall with legs stretched out in front of you
- bend the right knee and place the right foot on the ground to the left side of the left knee
- turn your shoulders so that you are facing to the right
- using your left arm against your right knee to help ease you further round
- use your right arm on the floor for support
- you will feel the stretch along the length of the spine and in the muscles around the right hip.

Quadriceps stretch

- lie face down on the floor, resting your forehead on your right hand
- press your hips firmly into the floor and bring your left foot up towards your buttocks
- take hold of the left foot with the left hand and ease the foot closer to your buttocks
- repeat with the right leg
- you will feel the stretch along the front of the thigh.

Brian Mackenzie

Module 4

Endurance

Introduction

Aerobic endurance

Aerobic fitness is primary for most sports. However, it is not the only fitness area and if it is focused on too much it can be detrimental to strength and power, which are equally, if not more, important in many sports. Trainers must think carefully about the fitness level they believe is appropriate for peak performance and then achieve that. For example, in elite football a high aerobic capacity is important, but for volleyball a moderate level will suffice. For most games, aerobic fitness governs how quickly one recovers between high-intensity sections and how much distance can be covered in a game.

Anaerobic endurance

During anaerobic (meaning without oxygen) work, involving maximum effort, the body is working so hard that the demands for oxygen and fuel exceed the rate of supply and the muscles have to rely on the stored reserves of fuel. In this situation waste products accumulate, the chief one being lactic acid. The muscles, being starved of oxygen, take the body into a state known as oxygen debt. The body's stored fuel soon runs out; activity ceases and will not be resumed until the lactic acid is removed and the oxygen debt repaid. Fortunately the body can resume limited activity after only a small proportion of the oxygen debt has been repaid.

Anaerobic endurance, important for many sports, can be developed by using repetition methods of relatively high-intensity work with limited recovery periods. Both the lactate system and the adenosine triphosphate – phosphate creatine (ATP-PC) system should be trained, but targeted in the correct proportions for each sport. For instance, tennis focuses almost solely on the ATP-PC system, due to short bursts and frequent rest play pattern, whereas squash requires significant lactate system training as play is much more continuous.

Overview of the endurance module

In this module we look at how you can develop your aerobic endurance to meet the demands of your sport.

- Brian Mackenzie explains how you can assess and improve your VO$_2$max.
- Frank Horwill explains how to develop your aerobic endurance with an example training programme.
- Raphael Brandon explains how swimmers should develop their aerobic endurance – quality is better than quantity.
- Raphael Brandon explains how a heart monitor can help you develop your aerobic endurance.

The articles in this module are applicable to most sports.

VO$_2$max

Introduction

Aerobic endurance can be measured by the volume of oxygen you can consume while exercising at your maximum capacity. VO$_2$max is the maximum amount of oxygen in millilitres that you can use in one minute, per kilogram of body weight. Those who are fit have higher VO$_2$max values and can exercise more intensely than those who are not as well conditioned.

Factors affecting VO$_2$max

The physical limitations that restrict the rate at which energy can be released aerobically are dependent upon:
- the chemical ability of the muscular cellular tissue system to use oxygen in breaking down fuels
- the combined ability of cardiovascular and pulmonary systems to transport the oxygen to the muscular tissue system.

Improving your VO$_2$max

Numerous studies show that you can increase your VO$_2$max by working out at an intensity that raises your heart rate to between 65% and 85% of its maximum for at least 20 minutes, three to five times a week. The following are samples of

Astrand's workouts for improving oxygen uptake:

1. Run at maximum speed for five minutes. Note the distance covered in that time. Assume that the distance achieved is 1900m. Rest for five minutes, and then run the distance (1900m) 20% slower, in other words in six minutes, with 30 seconds' rest, repeated many times. This is equal to your 10k pace.

2. Run at maximum speed for four minutes. Note the distance covered in that time. Rest for four minutes. In this case we will assume you run a distance of 1500m. Now run the same distance 15% slower, in other words in four minutes 36 seconds, with 45 seconds' rest, repeated several times.

3. Run at maximum effort for three minutes. Note the distance covered in that time. The distance covered is, say, 1000m. Successive runs at that distance are taken 10% slower or at 3 minutes 18 seconds, with 60 seconds' rest, repeated several times. This approximates to your 5k pace.

4. Run at maximum effort for five minutes. Note the distance covered in that time. The distance covered is, say, 1900m. Rest five minutes. Cover the distance 5% slower with one and a half minute's rest.

5. Run at maximum effort for three minutes. The distance covered is, say, 1100m. When recovered, run the same distance 5% slower, ie three minutes nine seconds, with one minute's rest, repeated several times.

It is suggested that in the winter, sessions 1 and 2 are done weekly, and in the track season, sessions 3, 4 and 5 are done weekly (by runners from 800m to the half marathon). Although it would be convenient to use the original distance marks made by the duration efforts, this does not take into account the athlete's condition before each session, so the maximum effort runs must be done on each occasion when they may be either more or less than the previous distance run.

The maximum duration efforts are in themselves quality sessions. If the pulse rate has not recovered to 120 beats-per-minute in the rest times given, the recovery period should be extended before the repetitions are started. The recovery times between the reps should be strictly adhered to. These workouts make a refreshing change from repetition running. When all five sessions are completed within a month, experience shows substantial improvements in performance.

Assessing your VO₂max (Cooper test)

Run for 12 minutes on a track, as fast as possible and record the distance covered. Calculate your VO₂max with the following algorithm:

- (Distance covered in metres - 504.9) / 44.73

Example: In 12 minutes you manage to run 3000m. This gives you an approximate VO₂max score of (3000-504.9)/44.73 = 55.8 ml/kg/min

Analyses of VO₂max scores

Female (values in ml/kg/min)

Age	Very Poor	Poor	Fair	Good	Excellent	Superior
13-19	<25.0	25.0 - 30.9	31.0 - 34.9	35.0 - 38.9	39.0 - 41.9	>41.9
20-29	<23.6	23.6 - 28.9	29.0 - 32.9	33.0 - 36.9	37.0 - 41.0	>41.0
30-39	<22.8	22.8 - 26.9	27.0 - 31.4	31.5 - 35.6	35.7 - 40.0	>40.0
40-49	<21.0	21.0 - 24.4	24.5 - 28.9	29.0 - 32.8	32.9 - 36.9	>36.9
50-59	<20.2	20.2 - 22.7	22.8 - 26.9	27.0 - 31.4	31.5 - 35.7	>35.7
60+	<17.5	17.5 - 20.1	20.2 - 24.4	24.5 - 30.2	30.3 - 31.4	>31.4

Male (values in ml/kg/min)

Age	Very Poor	Poor	Fair	Good	Excellent	Superior
13-19	<35.0	35.0 - 38.3	38.4 - 45.1	45.2 - 50.9	51.0 - 55.9	>55.9
20-29	<33.0	33.0 - 36.4	36.5 - 42.4	42.5 - 46.4	46.5 - 52.4	>52.4
30-39	<31.5	31.5 - 35.4	35.5 - 40.9	41.0 - 44.9	45.0 - 49.4	>49.4
40-49	<30.2	30.2 - 33.5	33.6 - 38.9	39.0 - 43.7	43.8 - 48.0	>48.0
50-59	<26.1	26.1 - 30.9	31.0 - 35.7	35.8 - 40.9	41.0 - 45.3	>45.3
60+	<20.5	20.5 - 26.0	26.1 - 32.2	32.3 - 36.4	36.5 - 44.2	>44.2

Ideal VO₂max scores for a selection of sports

VO₂max	Sport
>75 ml/kg/min	Middle distance Runners (male), Cyclists (male)
65 ml/kg/min	Squash (male)
60-65 ml/kg/min	Rowers (male), Football (male)
55 ml/kg/min	Swimmers (female), Runners (female)
55 ml/kg/min	Weight Lifters (male), Rugby (male)
50 ml/kg/min	Volleyball (female), Baseball (male)
45 ml/kg/min	Fencers (female)

Brian Mackenzie

When winter's coming, use this programme to boost your VO₂max

A 15-minute running test around a 400m track (Balke test) can lead to revolutionary improvements in fitness in just 12 weeks. The object of the 15-minute test is to cover as much distance as possible. A secondary factor is that the distance run can predict VO₂max with 95% accuracy. I tested a male runner this way and estimated his oxygen uptake as 64mls/kg/min. A week later he paid £40 for a sophisticated treadmill VO₂max test at a British Olympic Medical Centre; they gave him 65mls/kg/min.

For the technically minded, here are a few VO₂max predictions:

Distance Run	Predicted VO₂max (mls/kg/min)
4000m	56.5
4400m	61
4800m	65.5
5200m	70
5600m	75

As the distance run indicates current fitness levels, the same distance run can be used as a basis for further training. Let us imagine that an athlete runs exactly 4000m in 15 minutes. The target in 12 weeks' time is 4400m, which correlates to a 10% improvement in VO₂max. To achieve this, a minimum of four training sessions a week are required, which can be allocated on an every-other-day basis. Should a keen athlete decide on 12 sessions a week (twice-a-day training) there will be a correspondingly greater improvement in fitness, *ie* a greater distance run on the test.

Here is the procedure:

1. Run the test (in this example, 4000m in 15 minutes).
2. Halve the distance run on the test. In this case, 2000m. Once a week, run 4 x 2000m in 7.5 minutes with 60 seconds' recovery after each rep.
3. Double the distance run on the trial. In this example, 8000m (about five miles). Run this distance once a week in 33 minutes.
4. Calculate the time per lap. In this example, it is 90 seconds per 400m. (If the distance run was 5000m it would be 72 seconds/400m etc.) Halve this time (45 seconds), and subtract 8 seconds = 37 seconds. Once a week run a series of 200m repetitions in 37 seconds starting with 90 seconds' recovery, which decreases by 15 seconds after each 200m run, eg 37/90, 37/75, 37/60 down to 37/15. When you have reached the 15-second rest period, run the timed lap again and re-start from the beginning. Continue this until the time calculated cannot be recorded (either 200m in eight seconds, or 200m in 28 seconds).
5. Multiply the distance run on the original test by four, eg 4 x 4000m = 16k (about 10 miles). Run this distance once a week in 69 minutes.

The object of the exercise

The aim of all five of these training sessions is to improve the overall times each month. If the minimum volume is chosen, the sessions can be apportioned each week as follows:

Sunday: long run (4 x test run in 69 minutes or less).
Tuesday: repetition 200m with declining recovery.
Thursday: double-distance run (33 minutes).
Saturday: half the distance run x 4 with 60 seconds' recovery.

If the maximum volume is chosen each week, it is a good idea to do the double-distance run each morning and arrange the remaining sessions as above.

The physiological basis for this regime is as follows:
  1) The training is specifically designed to improve the distance run in 15 minutes. If this is achieved, VO_2max (fitness) will correspondingly improve.
  2) The world's leading work physiologists are agreed that VO_2max is best improved by running at between 80 and 100% of VO_2max.

To understand this we must remember the key:

Percentage of VO₂max	Related Pace
100	3k
95	5k
90	10k
80	Half marathon

We can now apply this key to each individual 3k and 5k pace (100-95% VO_2max). As fitness improves it will approach the latter more. Consider session three. This approaches the athlete's 10k speed (90% VO_2max). As fitness improves, it will also become a lactate response run in the range of 90% to 95% VO_2max. If we analyse session four, this approximates to the 1500m speed which is 110% VO_2max. Finally, session five is analogous to half marathon speed, as the 4 x the distance run improves from 69 minutes to 63 minutes, which will be 80% VO_2max.

What is a lactate-response-run?

I have mentioned that session three with improved fitness will become a lactate-response-run. Many athletes are mystified by this term. If a person goes for a jog, the amount of lactate circulating around the body will be negligible and the activity can continue for a very long time. If, however, the individual ran 800m full out, the body would be saturated in lactic acid, for no other middle-distance event produces so much saturation. This is why the great Olaf Astrand suggests that all runners should race 800m regularly, because they will be better able to cope with lesser amounts of lactate accumulated in longer and slower races.

In a lactate-response-run we do not want the former (jogging), nor do we desire the latter (800m speed). We require a point in our running speed just below the level where lactic acid begins to accumulate rapidly which we can maintain for four miles (6.5k). Now this cannot be our best 5k speed, nor is it our best 10k speed, for it will be too slow. It is between the two. When we get bogged down for some time with the same VO_2max figure, it is the lactate-response-run that will improve our fitness further with less likelihood of injury doing faster work on the track.

Jack Daniels has evolved a highly accurate table for response-run speeds based on an athlete's 3k time, and when compared to laboratory obtained lactate levels of elite athletes, it is identical with regard to speed per mile to be run.

Here is the table:

Best 3k Time	Suggested Lactate Response run (4 miles)
7 min 30 sec	4 min 16 sec/mile
8 min 30 sec	4 min 53 sec/mile
9 min 30 sec	5 min 40 sec/mile
10 min 30 sec	6 min 23 sec/mile
11 min 30 sec	7 min 05 sec/mile
12 min 30 sec	7 min 45 sec/mile

It is suggested that such runs are done over an exact mile circuit so that times can be monitored more easily. If you are a heart rate monitor enthusiast, a rough guide is that a lactate-response-run is not to be executed at less than 90% of maximum heart rate or more than 95% of maximum.

Start in the winter

After 12 weeks on the outlined programme a second test is carried out and the further distance covered must inevitably lead to new calculations resulting in progressively faster sessions. This type of training is best started in the winter and continued throughout the year, with modifications made to accommodate specific race requirements. For example, session two, 4 x half the distance run in 7.5 minutes, can be altered to 8 x a quarter of the distance run with three minutes 45 seconds' recovery. Session four, repetition 200m, can be altered to 400m reps at the same speed with the same recoveries as for the 200m. This, of course, will result in fewer reps being done.

So far we have discussed mainly aerobic fitness. The ability to sprint is a major asset in most sports. Basic speed is tested by running 40 yards (36.6m) full out from a standing or crouch start. The general goal is for males to get well below five seconds and for females to get well below six. Whatever figure is recorded, this can predict the potential 400m time with 95% accuracy using this formula: 40 yards time x 10 + 2 seconds = male 400m potential time; 40 yards time x 10 + 3 seconds = female 400m potential time. Thus a male who records exactly five seconds has the potential to run 400m in 52 seconds. A female who records six seconds has a potential 400m time of 63 seconds. When the 400m potential time has not been achieved, it is usually because sprint training repetitions have not exceeded 200m. The burning of sugar (glycolysis) in a 400m race starts after 300m, so work involving 350m full-out sprints is required.

Small amounts of sprint work done every other day in winter will get the reflexes toned up. All distance runners should have a sprint coach as well as their own distance running coach. To ignore this often leads to the athlete becoming a one-pace runner.

Frank Horwill

Why high-intensity training is a better model than high-volume training for swimmers, especially sprinters

It is probably fair to say that most swimmers and swim coaches see the number of hours spent in the pool as the main ingredient of swimming success and distances of 6k to 10k per day are not uncommon in elite swimming circles. Is this really the key to success, or is there an alternative approach that can produce even better results? This section aims to stir up the debate by suggesting that the traditional high-volume model of training will not optimise performance, especially for 100m and 200m swimmers.

This is written not from a swimming coach's perspective, but in the light of research on swim training. Scientific analysis of the demands of competitive swimming and running training methods has been shown to optimise performance. Swimmers should read on with open minds and may then choose to apply some of the principles to their own training programmes.

Research into the effects of high-volume swim training on performance suggests there is no advantage to piling on the kilometres. The legendary US physiologist Dave Costill has undertaken a great deal of research on swim training over the last three decades. In one study his team of scientists followed two groups of swimmers over a 25-week training period. Both groups began with once-daily training, but one group moved to twice-daily training in weeks 10 to 15, reverting to once-daily for the rest of the study period. At no stage of the 25-week training period did this group show enhanced performance or increased aerobic capacity as a result of their extra training. Basically, it was a waste of time.

In another study, Costill tracked the performance of competitive swimmers over a four-year period, comparing a group averaging 10k per day with a group averaging 5k per day, in relation to changes in competitive-performance-time over 100, 200, 500 and 1600m. Improvements in swim times were identical for both groups at around 0.8% per year for all events. Again, even though one group did twice as much training, both groups benefited to the same extent in the long-term.

To quote Costill directly: 'Most competitive swimming events last less than two minutes. How can training for three to four hours per day at speeds that are markedly slower than competitive pace prepare the swimmer for the maximal efforts of competition?'

Research from France supports Costill's conclusions. A team of scientists analysed the training and performance of competitive 100m and 200m swimmers over a 44-week period. Their findings were as follows:

- Most swimmers completed two training sessions per day.
- Swimmers trained at five specific intensities. These were swim speeds equivalent to two, four, six and a high 10mmol/L blood-lactate concentration pace and, finally, maximal sprint swimming.

- Over the whole season, the swimmers who made the biggest improvements were those who performed more of their training at higher paces. The volume of training had no influence on swim performance.

Feeling comfortable is not the point

The only conclusion to be drawn from this research is that faster and not longer training is the key to swimming success. Nevertheless, the high-volume, low-intensity training model probably remains the most common practice among elite swimmers, with even sprint swimmers focusing on clocking up the kilometres rather than more race-pace-specific training.

One of reasons for this high-volume bias is that swimmers and coaches believe that swimming technique, efficiency through the water and the 'feel' of the stroke are optimised by spending many hours in the pool. I have heard swimmers say they do not feel as comfortable in the water and confident about their technique unless they complete high doses of training. As a non-swimmer I am happy to admit my ignorance and to concede that the technical aspect of swim training is very important. However, the idea that high-volume training equates to superior race technique has no logical basis. If you told a 100m runner that the best way to optimise his sprint technique at maximum speed would be to complete many miles a week at 10k pace, you would be laughed off the track. Track sprinters focus on workouts and technical drills carried out at high intensity and positively avoid low-intensity/high-volume training in the belief that it inhibits power development.

The same must be true of swimming to a large extent. If a swimmer wants to increase stroke efficiency and technique during a competition, surely the best way to do this is to train at target race-pace. The more training time is spent at target race-pace, the more comfortable it will feel in competition. Dave Costill says: 'Large training volume prepares the athlete to tolerate a high volume of training but likely does little to benefit actual performance'. When swimmers talk of 'feeling comfortable' in the water, they may be referring to the sub-maximal speeds they perform in training, not the maximal efforts required in competition. Not only does high-volume training offer no benefit for swim performance, it may have negative effects. Two known consequences of high-volume training are depletion of glycogen muscle stores and fatigue of the fast-twitch muscle fibres, both of which will reduce the effectiveness of high-intensity race-pace training sessions and severely compromise any competitive performance.

Research has also shown that periods of high-volume training reduce the force production in the fast-twitch muscle fibres, which are essential for producing the fastest swim speeds. It has been shown that sprint swimmers have quite high proportions of fast-twitch muscles, over 60% in the deltoid and quadriceps. High-volume training does nothing for these fibres: indeed, it will dampen their force production by reducing the shortening velocity of the muscle contraction.

In this way, high-volume training can change fast-twitch fibres into those of the slow-twitch variety.

This probably explains why 'tapering' is so effective at improving performance for swimmers, as the fast-twitch fibres are able to recover during the period of low-volume training. It is known that maximal power increases after a tapering period, probably due to the fast-twitch fibres reproducing their high-velocity contraction properties. The French researchers mentioned above analysed the effects of tapering on swim performance and found that swimmers who used the most severe tapers, reductions of about half normal training volume, produced the biggest improvements in performance.

This begs the following questions:
- If such dramatic tapers in training are required to optimise performance, why are training volumes so high in the first place?
- Would it not be better for swimmers to develop power in a positive fashion during the training period?

Examination of the demands of sprint swimming events will help to answer these questions.

The metabolic demands of swimming

The shorter the swimming event, the greater the demand on the anaerobic energy systems. This is particularly true of the 50m, 100m and 200m events, lasting from around 20 to 120 seconds. The longer events, from 800m upwards, demand a larger contribution from the aerobic energy system. Evidence for this comes from blood-lactate concentrations following 100m and 200m competition swims, which are a very high 16 to 20mmol/L, suggesting that a great deal of energy is derived from the anaerobic breakdown of glycogen, resulting in lactic acid as a by-product. The highly anaerobic nature of sprint swim events would support the argument for higher-intensity and lower-volume training.

Some athletes and coaches go wrong by assuming it is best to do training that will reduce blood-lactate concentrations. This philosophy is based on the idea that high lactate is bad and will have a negative impact on performance. This leads to training programmes that focus on 'lactate threshold' training to improve the turnover of lactate and enhance the ability of the aerobic systems to produce more of the energy required for the event.

There are two problems with this model of training:
1) You need to be careful about assuming that a high lactate level is a bad thing. Remember that lactic acid is the by-product of anaerobic breakdown of glycogen. Lactic acid splits into the $H+$ ion and the lactate ion. It is the acidic $H+$ ion that is the bad guy, interfering with force production in the muscles and reducing the rate of glycolysis, thus slowing the athlete down. The

lactate ion simply diffuses through the muscle and into the bloodstream, with no evidence to suggest it has any negative impact on muscle function or energy production. In fact, the lactate ion can be recycled in the energy production cycle and used positively to help produce energy. So a high level of lactate in the blood is not bad in itself: it is simply an indicator that a lot of anaerobic energy production is occurring. The training adaptation you are seeking is not a reduction in lactate production, but rather an increase in the buffering of the H+ ion. Training at high intensities and so generating high levels of lactic acid helps the body get used to the increase in H+ in the muscles and improve its ability to buffer the acid.

2) Anaerobic glycolysis involves the fast breakdown of glycogen into energy-giving phosphates, while aerobic glycolysis involves a much slower breakdown. Without the anaerobic energy systems, maximal power and high speeds would be impossible, as the muscles would not get a fast enough supply of energy. If you want high power you have to have high levels of anaerobic energy supply.

For sprint swimming, anaerobic capacity is the good guy and it needs to be developed. If an event places great demands on the anaerobic system, the athlete needs to become more anaerobic. This may seem odd to those with traditional beliefs about training, but it is true. By focusing on high-volume aerobic training to reduce lactate levels you are in fact compromising your anaerobic fitness, which is the most important attribute for competitive success in sprint swimming.

For sprint swimmers, lactate threshold training geared to keeping lactate levels low is irrelevant. For swim distances up to and including 200m, the accumulation of high levels of lactate does not matter: indeed, it is probably a good thing as it reflects a good anaerobic capacity. For longer events, such as 800m and 1500m, where the aerobic system is much more important, lactate threshold training would be relevant, as swimmers need to maintain an intensity level for much longer, relying on the aerobic energy system.

The race-pace model of training

The implication of all the research mentioned above is that spending more training time at high-intensity levels, at and above race-pace, will offer greater benefits than swimming lots of kilometres per day at much slower than race speeds.

In the world of running, thanks to the influence of pioneering physiologists and coaches such as Frank Horwill, Veronique Billat, Jack Daniels and Owen Anderson, the focus of training is now on 'pace' rather than lactate levels or heart rates. By using pace to monitor the intensity of training, the athlete is switching into a performance mentality, ensuring the training is specific to the competitive event.

Middle-distance running coach Frank Horwill created a five-pace system of training, which involves performing regular, quality training sessions at two paces higher than race-pace, race-pace itself and two paces slower than race-pace. If you are a 1500m runner, you will complete interval workouts at 400m, 800m, 1500m, 5000m and 10,000m race-paces. This model of training breeds a philosophy that values high-intensity ahead of high-volume.

The coaches referred to above also recognise that different events call for different kinds of training. The 5k running event, which takes about 12 to 15 minutes, requires a high proportion of aerobic training and 5k-pace-specific workouts, while the 800m event, lasting about two minutes, requires a high proportion of anaerobic training and 800m-pace workouts. I would argue that this kind of training model would serve competitive swimmers much better than the traditional high-volume approach.

There is evidence that the difference between swimmers who reach the Olympics and those who do not is due more to the distance achieved per stroke than to stroke frequency. The way to increase your distance per stroke is to increase the force generated by the active muscles and achieve an optimum position in the water. This is best achieved by high-intensity training, with the aim of developing power in the water at race-pace.

How can swimmers change their training to enhance power at pace speeds?

Again, there may be lessons to learn from running. The 100m swim takes about 50 seconds, so is similar to the 400m track event; the 200m swim takes about 110 seconds and so is analogous to the 800m running race. It may therefore be possible for swimmers to improve their performances by modelling their training on that of middle-distance and long sprint track athletes.

For example, an international 800m runner will carry out a preparation period of aerobic capacity training with continuous running at 10k pace and slower, plus interval training at 5k pace. The 200m swimmer's equivalent could be the usual high-volume training programme.

This base training phase will be followed by more specific training, with more 5k and 10k pace runs and some more interval workouts for the anaerobic system, at 800m and 1500m pace, probably about three times a week. The 200m swimmer's equivalent could be to maintain a fairly high volume but include more above-lactate-threshold-pace workouts and race-pace or close to race-pace interval workouts three times a week: for example, 10 x 100m at 400m race-pace, with 60 seconds' rest.

This phase is followed by a very intense pre-competition phase of training, the goal of which is to maximise the athlete's anaerobic capacity. Aerobic training is cut to a minimum maintenance level, and high-intensity anaerobic sessions at 400m, 800m, and 1500m paces performed about five to six times a week. For the swimmer, this could involve a morning swim at an easy lactate-threshold pace or below, with very high-quality race-pace and faster-than-race-pace interval workouts in the evening. For example, eight x 50m at 200m race-pace, with 60-seconds rest.

The competition phase for runners will simply maintain aerobic and anaerobic fitness with maintenance training and plenty of recovery between races. For the swimmer this could involve some 'aerobic' slow-speed workouts and some race-pace and sprint workouts, probably limiting training to five to six times per week. The best middle-distance runners probably perform a maximal sprint workout once a week throughout the year to keep speed up to scratch. Swimmers could also incorporate this into their programmes with, for example, 10 x turn into 20m max sprint with three minutes rest, once a week.

I have argued, based on research, analysis of the energy demands of swimming races and the training methods of comparable athletes, that it is best for swimmers to focus on high-intensity rather than high-volume training. More specifically, swimmers would benefit from plenty of race-pace training to develop power and efficiency in the water at the speeds they use in competition.

Raphael Brandon

How to use heart rate to quantify your fitness training intensity

Articles in *Peak Performance* often detail elite and complex aerobic training methods to boost endurance performance, VO_2max and lactate threshold. These articles typically refer to target training intensities and heart rates to achieve, say, a new 10k or marathon best. They recommend high-intensity training, with very high target heart rates, to complement the longer 'steady state' sessions at more moderate intensities.

However, using target training intensities and heart rates is also useful for those of us whose aerobic training is aimed at improving general health and fitness, or as general conditioning for a recreational sport. In this more modest form, aerobic training involves an endurance activity, such as cycling, running or rowing, performed continuously for a certain amount of time, usually 20 to 30 minutes. It is recommended that if this kind of activity is performed three to five times a week, it will bring about optimum benefits. Obviously if you do more you will get fitter, but as a general rule, three to five x 20 to 30 minutes a week yields a good fitness reward for the amount of time invested, and so is optimal for general fitness needs.

It is also advisable that, with this kind of aerobic training, the exercise intensity should be moderately hard. The American College of Sports Medicine (ACSM) officially recommends that the optimal intensity is between 60% and 80% of VO₂max. VO₂max is the maximum amount of oxygen, in millilitres, one can use in one minute per kilogram of bodyweight. It is the standard measure of aerobic fitness. However, it is impossible to maintain maximal oxygen use for longer than about eight to 10 minutes. Thus, for general fitness training, one should aim to be at 60% to 80% of maximum capacity and maintain this level for 20 to 30 minutes. This intensity is comparable to the training levels elite athletes would use on their 'steady state' sessions. When performing some of the more advanced interval sessions, elite athletes will be at intensities greater than 85% VO₂max. At the other extreme, activity at an intensity of 40% VO₂max is likely to improve health but will not significantly improve aerobic fitness.

Take the case of Joe

It is possible to estimate your exercise intensity as a percentage of VO₂max from your training heart rate. This is very useful, for elite and recreational athlete alike, because by monitoring your heart rate you can quantify your training effort and target the correct intensity for maximum benefits. These calculations are possible because of the linear relationship between heart rate (HR) and oxygen use (VO₂) with increasing rates of work. For example, if Joe is sitting down doing nothing, his resting HR might be 70bpm. At this HR, VO₂ would be at its baseline level, which is approximately 3.5 ml/kg/min. If Joe starts to walk, his HR may increase to around 100bpm as the VO₂ goes up to cope with the extra energy demand. If Joe now breaks into a jog, his HR will go higher again, up to 140bpm, say, as VO₂ increases further. Then, if Joe runs as fast as he can for three minutes, his HR might go up to its maximum of 190bpm. At this point Joe will have reached his VO₂max. Therefore, at VO₂max, HR is also at maximum and at a percentage of VO₂max, there is a corresponding percentage of HRmax. This relationship has been shown to hold true across sex, age and exercise type. The ACSM suggests a correlation that looks like this:

VO₂max	HRmax
40%	55%
60%	70%
80%	85%
85%	90%

These values are derived from various studies which have compared VO₂ with HR and determined regression equations for percentage HRmax versus percentage VO₂max.

Revising the ACSM formula

These target values of percentage HRmax provide a means of quantifying exercise intensity to optimise training results. If the optimal training intensity is 60% to 80% of VO₂max, then according to the ACSM the corresponding optimal training HR is 70% to 85% of HRmax. However, the ACSM made these official recommendations in 1991. Since then, a study by David Swain and his US-based research team has criticised the mathematical methods used to derive the regression equations in previous research. Using more correct statistical procedures, they re-examined the relationship between percentage VO_2max and percentage HRmax and found that the ACSM formula underestimates HR at the target values of percentage VO_2max. Their results led to a regression equation of *percentage of HRmax* = 0.64 x % VO_2max + 37. This produces the following figures:

VO₂max	HRmax
40%	63%
60%	75%
80%	88%
85%	92%

Therefore, using these results, the optimal training HR range for general aerobic fitness is 75% to 88% HRmax, significantly higher than the 70% to 85% HRmax from the ACSM. For Joe, with his HRmax at 190bpm, using Swain et al's method, his target HR range is 143 to 168bpm, as opposed to the ACSM's recommended range of 133 to 161bpm. The improved research from Swain et al thus suggests that the training HR should be pushed up a little to 75% to 88% HRmax to bring about optimum results.

For elite athletes, Swain et al showed that percentage HRmax for the same percentage VO_2max were slightly higher compared to average. Therefore, for steady state training, an HR range of 77% to 89% VO_2max would be appropriate for an elite athlete. For advanced interval training, the intensity must be above 85% VO_2max or above 92% HRmax. For example, during a session comprising 6 x 800m runs at 5k pace, the training intensity will be at 90% to 95% VO_2max. This would correspond to a training HR of 95% to 97% HRmax.

We can see clearly from these examples that knowing accurately what percentage HRmax corresponds to a target percentage VO_2max is very useful for both the average and the elite athlete. By using the formula derived by Swain et al, we can calculate a target training heart rate for the particular goal of the individual. So, how precisely is HRmax calculated?

The easiest and best-known method is to use the formula *220 – age*. This is the method recommended in the ACSM guidelines. However, the actual derivation for this regression equation has never been published. It is used since it is a simple way to get a good estimate of HRmax. In an attempt to be more accurate, numerous cross-sectional studies have been done to investigate the relationship between HRmax, age and other factors. A paper by Londeree and Moeschberger from the University of Missouri, Columbia, collates the data from all these studies in order to bring together the findings.

What they show is that HRmax varies mostly with age, but the relationship is not a linear one. Thus the 220 – age formula is slightly inaccurate. For adults under 30, it will overestimate HRmax and for adults over 45 it will underestimate HRmax. This is especially true for well trained over-45s whose max HR does not reduce as much as with sedentary individuals of the same age. Londeree and Moeschberger suggest an alternative formula of *206.3 – (0.711 x age)*. Similarly, Miller et al from Indiana University propose the formula *217 – (0.85 x age)* as a suitable HRmax calculation. In my experience, it is the Miller formula which gives appropriate estimates when calculating HRmax from age alone.

Swimming heart rates are lower

Londeree and Moeschberger also looked at other variables to see if these had an effect on HRmax. They found that neither sex nor race make any difference. However, HRmax does vary with activity and fitness level. Studies have shown that HRmax on a treadmill is consistently five to six beats higher than on a bicycle ergometer and two to three beats higher than on a rowing ergometer. Heart rates while swimming are significantly lower still, around 14bpm, than for treadmill running. Running and Versaclimber show similar HRmax.

Londeree and Moeschberger also found fitness levels lead to a variation in HRmax. Elite endurance athletes and moderately trained individuals will have an HRmax three or four beats lower than a sedentary individual. However, as already stated, this is only true for young athletes; well trained over-50s are likely to have a higher HRmax than that which is average for their age.

This is of utmost relevance to those using the rower or bicycle or those who are very fit, since training HRs will have to be calculated differently. To do this, Londeree and Moeschberger offer us another formula, a slightly more complicated interactive equation to calculate HRmax for different ages, activities and fitness levels. However, it is very difficult to use without a calculator and a degree in mathematics! (The details are at the end of this article.)

My own suggestion

Having outlined various methods for calculating HRmax, I would recommend the following, which combines the Miller formula with the research from Londeree and Moeschberger. Use the Miller formula of HRmax = 217 – 0.85 x age for running and Versaclimber training with average trainees.

- Subtract three beats for rowing training.
- Subtract five beats for bicycle training.
- Subtract three beats from these estimates for elite athletes under 30.
- Add two beats for 50 year-old elite athletes and add four beats for 55+ years.

Here is a chart to help you.

age	run/ climb		row		bike	
	average	elite	average	elite	average	elite
20	200	197	197	194	195	192
25	196	193	193	190	191	188
30	192	189	189	186	187	184
35	187	187	184	184	182	182
40	183	183	180	180	178	178
45	179	179	176	176	174	174
50	175	177	172	174	170	172
55	170	174	167	171	165	169
60	166	170	163	167	161	165

One question that you may be justified in asking is, who cares? Will all these complicated percentages and formulae actually make a difference, when the old ACSM recommendations are so straightforward? The point is that, if you want to use heart rate monitors, it serves little purpose unless you know *accurately* what training intensity the measurement represents. For example, a 45 year-old jogging to get fit should maintain 60% VO$_2$max for 20 to 30 minutes' continuous run. Using the old ACSM recommendations, they would be aiming for 70% HRmax. HRmax would be estimated at 175bpm, using the 220 – age formula. This gives a target training HR of 123bpm. However, the jogger's HRmax is more likely to be 179bpm and, following Swain et al, target training HR should be 75% HRmax. These two changes give a revised training HR of 134bpm, a massive 11bpm difference in target HR. If our 45-year-old had followed the old recommendations, their training would have been below optimal intensity, at 50% VO$_2$max, and they would not have got the most from the invested training time.

These inaccuracies can also disadvantage the elite athlete. For example, a 25 year-old elite cyclist using the 220 – age formula may think his HRmax is 195bpm. However, it is more likely to be only 188bpm. This could mean he is overestimating target training HR for certain sessions, which can be undesirable if mileage rather than intensity is the aim of the session.

The take-home message of this article is a word of warning if you use traditional calculations to quantify training intensities. If 60% VO$_2$max is the minimum intensity for aerobic fitness improvements, then 75% and not 70% HRmax is the minimum training target HR. However, using a range of 75% to 88% HRmax for training targets is probably best. To calculate HRmax, the simple 220 – age formula is not always accurate. The alternative formulas provided will give you more accurate estimates.

For beginners and individuals training for a healthy fitness level, or for a recreational sport, I recommend that you calculate your HRmax for your chosen training activity and then the 75% HRmax training target. During your workouts, use an HR monitor or take your pulse and make sure that you put in enough effort to get your HR to the required level for a fitness benefit.

For elite athletes, use the new formulae to accurately calculate your maximum and target heart rates. Remember, tough interval sessions need to be really tough, so make sure your HR reaches around 95% HRmax. However, sometimes you need to keep training moderate, so aim for 77% to 89% HRmax for steady-state training.

Summary data

Target intensity for health benefits = 40% VO₂max = 63% HRmax
Target intensity for aerobic fitness = 60-80% VO₂max = 75-88% HRmax
Target intensity for elite training = >85% VO₂max = >92% HRmax

Swain et al equation: % HRmax = 0.64 x % VO₂max + 37
Miller et al formula: HRmax = 217 - (0.85 x age)
Londeree & Moeschberger interactive formula: training HRmax =
199.1 + 0.119 x AEF4 + 0.112 x AE + 6.28 x EF3 + 3.485 x F2 + 2.468 - 0.0006 x A4 - 0.591 x A

A = age; A4 = (age 4)/1000; E = exercise type,
If run = 1, if bike = 0;
If sedentary F2 = 1, otherwise F2 = 0;
If active F3 = 1, otherwise F3 = 0;
If endurance trained F4 = 1, otherwise F4 = 0

Raphael Brandon

References

Swain et al (1994), 'Target HR for the development of CV fitness', *Medicine & Science in Sports & Exercise,* 26(1), pp112-116

Londeree and Moeschberger (1982), 'Effect of age and other factors on HRmax', *Research Quarterly for Exercise & Sport,* 53(4), pp297-304

Miller et al (1993), 'Predicting max HR', *Medicine & Science in Sports & Exercise,* 25(9), pp1077-1081

Brahler and Blank (1995), 'Versaclimber elicits higher VO₂max than treadmill running or rowing ergometry', *Medicine & Science in Sports & Exercise,* 27(2), pp249-254

ACSM Position Stand (1990), 'The recommended quantity and quality of exercise for developing and maintaining cardiorespiratory and muscular fitness in healthy adults', *Medicine & Science in Sports & Exercise,* 22: pp265-274

Module 5

Strength

Introduction

The common definition of strength is the ability to exert a force against a resistance. The strength needed for a sprinter to explode from the blocks is different to the strength needed by a weightlifter to lift a 200kg dumbbell. This implies that there are different types of strength. The classifications of strength are:

- maximum strength – the greatest force that is possible in a single maximum contraction
- elastic strength – the ability to overcome a resistance with a fast contraction
- strength endurance – the ability to express force many times over.

A muscle will only strengthen when it is worked beyond its normal operation - when it is overloaded.

Overview of the strength module

In this module we look at various methods of improving strength, and provide examples of possible training sessions.

- Raphael Brandon examines how to develop your maximum strength with weight training and, at the end of the module, how to develop your elastic strength with complex training (a mix of plyometrics and weights).
- John Shepherd explains how to develop a weights programme specific to your chosen sport.
- Walt Reynolds shows how to improve elastic strength with medicine balls and how to develop your strength endurance with circuit training.
- Brian Mackenzie explains how to develop your elastic strength with plyometrics.

The articles in this module are applicable to most sports.

How to develop maximum strength

The aim of this article is to outline how to design your strength routines, in terms of intensity and content, to make sure you get the optimum gains in strength for the time spent in the gym. I will begin by discussing the best intensity and volume for strength improvements. However, throughout the article I will be discussing maximum strength-training methods, which are not the same as bodybuilding. Currently, by far the most common strength-training format would be three sets of eight to 12 repetitions of each exercise. Give or take a few minor variations on a theme, this is generally what you would see when watching many gym routines. Recently, however, research has questioned this practice of three sets of each exercise. For example, Feigenbaum and Pollock (1997) reviewed eight well controlled studies comparing variations in sets of strength routines. No studies showed two sets to be significantly superior to one, and only one study showed three sets to be significantly superior to one or two.

In the light of this, when the American College of Sports Medicine published its latest *Position Stand on Health and Fitness Training*, it recommended adults should perform one set of eight to 12 repetitions, two to three times per week, for optimum strength benefits. You may be surprised at this. Only one set? What good will that do? However, we have to examine exactly what the ACSM specifies, and I quote: 'one set of eight to 12RM or to near fatigue should be completed ... or for older persons, one to 15RM may be more appropriate.'

What this means

The key element of this recommendation is that the resistance intensity has been clearly defined as eight to 12RM. RM stands for the Repetition Maximum and refers to the number of repetitions that can be performed before fatigue inhibits the completion of a further repetition with correct form. (When we get tired we can always force a few extra ones by cheating on the technique, but this does not count when assessing RM.)

The following example should make this clear. A male athlete is tested for his bench press performance. After a warm-up trial on a suitably easy weight, plus a couple of minutes' rest, he is given a 60kg bar to bench. He performs nine repetitions with correct technique but just fails while attempting to push up the 10th repetition and requires a little assistance. Thus 60kg is the 10RM load for this athlete. According to the ACSM, this makes 60kg an ideal training weight for strength development, and if he performed one set at 60kg two to three times a week he should significantly improve his bench-press strength. After a few sessions he will be able to complete 10 repetitions without assistance, then 11 repetitions and then 12. By this stage, 60kg has become his 12RM load. To ensure the best results and to stay within the ACSM guidelines, our athlete now needs to put the weight up. This is because, for maximum strength gains, the optimal range has been proven to be eight to 12RM, or even four to eight RM for power sports. Decreasing the relative load from 12 to 20RM would favour the development of muscular endurance and muscle toning.

The key is the RM value

Thus when designing strength exercises the most important variable is the RM value for each exercise. The number of sets performed at this level seems to be less influential. As long ago as 1962, Berger showed that 12 weeks of three-times-a-week training produced a 22% increase in bench-press strength with one set of six to 10RM, 22% increase from two sets of six to 10RM and 25% increase from three sets of six to 10RM – hardly a major difference for three times as much volume. Results like this are also found in more recent studies of both upper and lower body exercises.

When you next design a strength programme, instead of three sets of eight to 12 repetitions, try one set of eight to 12RM. There is a subtle but significant difference between eight to 12 repetitions and eight to 12RM, since the latter specifies the intensity of the training. Remember that it is the intensity and not the volume of the weight training that has the largest influence on its effectiveness. As Feigenbaum and Pollock have said recently (1999): 'One common factor in all effective strength programmes is the inclusion of at least one set of the maximal or near maximal number of repetitions for each exercise performed.'

Popular practice for athletes is to perform the usual three sets of 10, using a weight that allows the first set to be moderate, the second to feel a bit tough and the third very difficult or to fatigue. However, while this satisfies the above recommendation that at least one set is maximal, the weight intensity is probably too low. If our athlete trains at a weight intensity where he can complete three sets of 10, I would estimate that this weight intensity is at least his 15RM load, and maybe higher. This places the training intensity outside the optimum range for strength results. If we go back to our earlier bench presser, instead of the newly recommended one set to maximum at 60kg, he would perform three sets of 10 at around 45kg to 50kg. The chances are the former will give him a greater return in strength gains from less time invested.

The reason for multiple sets

So why do we all do three sets of 10 when a single set of 10RM will do just as well, if not better? What we need to remember is that, unfortunately, research studies often last no more than three months and often involve moderately trained subjects. Both the length of the training schedule and the status of the athlete are crucial to the outcome of the training programme. In other words, to be strictly correct, it is only proven that one set of eight to 12RM is best for moderately trained subjects for an initial training period.

Thus, multiple-set training programmes are recommended to ensure that the training stimulus is progressive and will continue to stress the body sufficiently so as to produce further strength improvements. Multiple-set programmes are probably most suitable. However, just because you feel you need the extra volume that multiple sets provide, do not forget that you must stay within the optimum intensity range of four to 12RM. Practically, this means the athlete still performs each set to the maximum and takes generous rest periods to allow for multiple sets. For example, our aforementioned bench presser has now decided to up the volume of his workouts. Let us say he was currently performing one set at 65kg, which was his 10RM load. To perform a second set, he would need three to five minutes' rest. If he only took one minute's rest, having just completed one maximum set, he would be unlikely to perform more than five repetitions the second time round. Intensity is the key, so, if you do not take enough rest, you will not be able to push enough weight. Remember that there is no point increasing to multiple sets if you end up decreasing to a sub-optimal intensity. Thus the recommended protocol for multiple sets for strength gains would be two to four sets of four to 12 RM with three to five minutes' rest.

Practical issues

So far we have established, in theory, the most effective design for strength improvements. The crucial point is that the training load must be within the four to 12RM range. Initially, one set to maximum will be sufficient, but for long-term improvement for elite athletes multiple sets will be required. Having established the theory, let us now look at a few practical issues regarding the content of the workout to ensure that our strength routines are fully effective. These issues are: exercise selection, exercise order and warm-up sets.

The main point about exercise selection is the athlete's training goal. The content of the workout must relate directly to the desired training effect. The goals may vary greatly, depending on the athlete's sport, position or event. There are too many possible variations to be covered here, but I will give some examples to illustrate the point and try to pass on some useful tips.

If the training goal is for general strength development, I would suggest selecting about eight exercises that involve large muscle groups and cover as much of the body as possible. For example, the following eight exercises cover pretty well all major muscle groups: leg press, leg curls, bench press, lat pull-downs, biceps curls, triceps press, ab crunch and back extension. One would perform sets of eight to 12RM of each of these exercises.

Sport-related training

If the strength training is related to a sport, the choice of exercises must be functional. This is because training effects are very specific. To ensure that the strength you develop in the gym brings about an improvement in performance, the strength exercise must be biomechanically related to the sporting movements. This is known as the 'carry-over effect'. For example, squats are a functional exercise because they train the quads, hamstrings and gluteals in a way that is related to running and jumping. In contrast, the knee extension exercise involves only knee extension, training the quads in isolation. This has no functional relevance to running or jumping, so improving your strength on this exercise will not improve your ability to run or jump. It may, however, improve your ability to kick.

Free weights are also considered more functional because the athlete has to use the synergistic small muscles to stabilise the movement as well as the large prime-mover muscles to execute the movement. This means, for example, that an exercise such as the dumbbell lunge, if performed with correct technique encouraging good alignment and upper body pressure, should develop body core stability as well as leg strength. This also highlights the point that quality technique and instruction are paramount for optimum strength improvements.

Do not forget muscle balance

Another practical point to consider in exercise selection is muscle balance. It is essential that both sides of the body are developed evenly and that opposing muscle groups have the correct relative strength to each other. Any imbalances may lead to injury or instability during sports movements. For this reason, you should always design workouts that result in balanced strength development. For instance, with every upper body push or press exercise also include a row or pull exercise. With some sports, a major goal of strength training is to redress imbalances between sides. For example, tennis players often have a dominant arm and uneven trunk strength. One solution to this would be choosing exercises that work each side individually, thus giving the weaker side a chance to catch up.

Exercise order...

The final practical point regarding exercise selection is the order of the exercises in the workout. It is recommended that large muscle group exercises and the most important exercises in the workout should precede small muscle or single joint exercises. For example, a sprinter may be using this type of programme:

- power clean
- squats
- bench press
- dumbbell lunge
- lat pull-down
- lateral raise
- bent-over lateral raise
- triceps press
- twisted crunch.

The power clean and squats come first because they are the most functionally important exercises for the sprinter. The power clean precedes the squat because technically it is a more difficult movement. The bench, lat pull and lunge come next because they all involve large muscle mass. The shoulder and triceps exercises come next because they are single-joint movements. The twisted crunch comes last because trunk strength is always required for good stability and technique in any exercise. Thus the trunk exercises should come at the end of a routine so that trunk muscle fatigue does not compromise technique during other exercises.

...and warm-up

The correct warm-up is also essential if weight training is to be fully effective. I recommend starting with some easy aerobic activity for about five minutes, particularly a rowing machine because it involves both upper and lower body. The next stage of the warm-up would be a choice of active mobility exercises for the whole body. The purpose of these exercises is to take each major joint through its active range of motion without any loading before the workout begins.

The most important element of warming up for strength training is to perform warm-up sets before each new muscle group or movement is trained. The purpose of warm-up sets is to gradually prepare the muscle for the maximal intensity loads to come. Remember that if you want to perform sets of four to 12RM, it means going to maximum. The correct load for the warm-up set would be about 60% of the training weight.

It is best to perform each of these warm-up sets immediately before the exercise. For example, a sprinter following the routine outlined above would start his workout with a warm-up set of power cleans. Then he would perform his training set of power cleans. He would not need a warm-up set for squats because the power clean movement would be sufficient. He would then precede both bench press and lat pull-downs with a warm-up set. The lunges, shoulder and triceps exercises would not require warm-up sets because the muscles involved would be already warm from the large multi-muscle exercises that preceded them. This is another important reason for putting large muscle mass exercises first in the routine order.

Note that there are no stretching exercises involved in the warm-up. Despite their popularity, stretching exercises are not proven to be an effective part of a warm-up. In fact, stretching may actually be inappropriate for strength training because it relaxes the muscles, reducing force development potential by inhibiting the stretch reflex.

In summary, to optimise strength gains design your workouts so that you train at the four to 12RM intensity and take long rests to facilitate multiple sets to maximum. Think carefully about the exercises included in your workout, asking if they are functionally relevant to your training goal and whether they will promote muscle balance and stability. Finally, design the workout using the most appropriate order of exercises so that the most important muscles are training first and the correct warm-up procedures are used.

Raphael Brandon

References

Feigenbaum and Pollock (1999), *Med Sci Sp & Ex*, vol 31, pp38-45
Feigenbaum and Pollock (1997), *Phys. Sportsmed*, vol 25, pp44-64
ASCM Position Stand (1998), *Med Sci Sp & Ex*, vol 30, pp975-991

For sporting success make your weights programme specific to your chosen activity

These days, hardly any sports performers can afford to neglect weight training. At the Manchester Commonwealth Games, even England's crown green lawn bowlers had weight-trained to improve their performance. Get this training right and you could find your place on the medal rostrum; get it wrong and you could end up at the back of the field.

Weight training for endurance

It has long been accepted that weight training (and the right strength-training programme) can improve performance for aerobic athletes. Take swimming: depending on the stroke, the arms and legs contribute different amounts of power to propel the swimmer through the water. Freestyle, for example, requires an upper body contribution of 70% and a lower body contribution of 30%. By strengthening the muscles that move the shoulder girdle, upper arm and forearm, hips and legs, it follows that, everything else being equal, performance will be improved.

But it is crucial to select the right exercises, perform them at the right intensity and place them within a progressive and carefully structured weights programme. Olympic rowing coach Terry O'Neill believes that a weight-training programme for his sport should mirror actual race requirements as closely as possible (a principle that should always be adhered to regardless of sport). This means that:

1. the exercises selected must be relevant to rowing
2. they must be performed ultimately at a pace equivalent to the actual stroke
3. they must create conditions that mirror the heart rate levels sustained during a 2k race
4. they must reflect the time it takes to complete the race distance.

In his most specific six-week weight-training microcycle, O'Neill reduces the amount of weight the rowers attempt to between 15kg and 30kg. This is so that they can complete 45 seconds of continuous rhythmic exercise at a similar rate to the stroke in a race.

At the end of each station, the athlete moves on to the next exercise without stopping, providing a total of eight minutes of work, during which time the heart rate will rise to 85% to 95% of maximum (see Table 1 on page 83 for exercises).

O'Neill gets the athletes to rest for two minutes at the end of each circuit and the aim is for them to complete three of these circuit workouts per week during the first three weeks and four in weeks four, five and six of this microcycle. The specific exercises utilised are: high pulls, press behind neck, front curl, bent-over rowing, lateral dips (side bends) to right and left, squat, bench press, clean and press, jack-knife crunch, bench pull and hyper extensions.

The sport-specific transference from this microcycle appears considerable. By targeting primarily type I muscle fibres and the cardiovascular system, an intense physiological response would be elicited, similar to that achieved during a high-intensity, interval-style rowing workout.

This workout should also avoid the 'physiological confusion' that can arise from targeting two different physiological goals, *eg* strength and endurance, at the same time. (Note that it was designed for indoor rowing but was adapted from O'Neill's vast knowledge of on-water-rowing training.)

Weight training for speed/power: why bigger is not always best

Lifting progressively heavier weights will not in itself lead to improved power and speed, but many athletes and coaches still get caught up with this 'heavier and bigger is best' strategy. Too much bulk is just that: an additional load to transport around the track or into the air. If increased muscle size on its own brought the required results, then a body builder would be able to run as fast as 2002 100m world record-holder Tim Montgomery.

It is how you develop the size and strength and where you take it to after and during a gross strength development phase, that counts. A larger (and stronger) muscle will exert greater force and ultimately more power, but simply pushing out near maximum repetition lifts, repetition after repetition, without sport-specific channelling is a waste of time.

So how should you weight-train for explosive power?

Charles Van Commenee is UK athletics' multi-events and jumps coach and it was he who coached Denise Lewis to Sydney gold. He believes that to develop power you initially need a good strength base, and advocates the use of exercises that train the whole body. Intensity is set at 90% of one repetition maximum (1RM) and his athletes perform five to 15 sets, but only using one to two repetitions and interspersed by long recovery periods of three to four minutes.

After a couple of months' training this way, the athletes move on to a power development phase, lifting at 70% to 85% of 1RM. The number of sets performed depends on the stage of the training year, but varies between three and six. At 70% of 1RM, five repetitions are performed, and at 85%, three. As before, a good recovery is crucial to unimpaired performance.

Van Commenee explains his training methodology in terms of a specific hormonal response. At a high percentage of 1RM, testosterone is released, boosting the speed development that his athletes need. At lower percentages and using multiple repetitions (8 – 10), growth hormone release tends to predominate, which is good for general muscle building but less advantageous for power athletes whose power-to-weight ratio is crucial.

Again, as with our rowing weight-training plan, it is crucial to select exercises that have a real relevance to the sport in question, particularly during the power development phase. The direct transference of, for example, a power clean to a high jump take-off is marginal and much less direct than the physiological responses elicited by our rowing schedule.

Table 1

Exercise	Sports applicable	Sport-specific value (Why?)
Split squat with the front foot on a wobble board/medicine ball	Field sports, jumping events, running	Elicits a proprioceptive ability; improves balance and strength; can reduce injury by preparing legs for 'unstable' force transference
Single arm dumbbell bench presses/shoulder press from a fit ball	Running, field sports	The key here is the role that the core performs in having to 'straitjacket' power transference
Sprint arm action with light dumbbells	Running	Develops a powerful and technically correct arm drive
Lunges/step-up drives	Running	Although not as specific as the other moves, it follows that, as running uses one leg at a time, weight training with one leg at a time will have a greater training transference

A power clean cannot be performed at the speed of a high jump take-off, nor could the same amount of force be overcome and nor, of course, could it be performed on one leg after a curved approach to a bar.

Weight training for speed (and endurance) obviously has certain limitations. It can only take an athlete so far, and more specialised exercises like plyometrics, sports specific drills and the sport itself must be used to channel the strength gained through weight training directly into improved performance.

Weight training and open sports skills: strengthening the body

Swimming, rowing and sprinting are predominantly 'closed skills', requiring the same movement pattern to be repeated over and over again. However, football, rugby, tennis and other field or court sports require myriad 'open sports skills'. And it is in these sports that the direct contribution of weight training to performance can appear less relevant. A tennis player reacts to a serve, a goalkeeper to a shot and weight training is unlikely to condition a directly transferable movement pattern. Why? The speed of movement, balance, proprioception and specific sport skills are incredibly specific to the requirement of the movements.

So what is the role of weight training for these sports? The answer is twofold:
1. to strengthen the body and protect it from injury by strengthening tendons, ligaments and muscles (a further reason for endurance athletes to weight train)
2. to provide a base for better (stronger/less fatigued/faster) open skill performance.

Mike Antoniades, a specialist speed, power and weight-training coach who has worked with many top sportsmen and women using the Frappier Acceleration system (see earlier module), provides a further third reason why the open skills performer should not neglect weight training. He notes that footballers can lose up to 35% of their strength during a season and more if they are unlucky enough to sustain an injury. The open skills performer therefore needs a weight-training programme that maintains specific strength across a season.

Sport-specific weight-training exercises and their value

Table 1 includes highly specific weight-training exercises. Some, like the first, even contain an element of open sports skill performance because the performer has not just to perform the move but also to balance and be spatially aware.

This is similar to the requirements of a striker having to take a shot at goal while off-balance. Note that these are advanced moves and should only be attempted by well conditioned athletes who have a suitable level of prior conditioning.

Six top weight-training tips for enhancing sports performance
1. Do some 'muscle re-education' work after lifting. If you are a cyclist, for example, you could do three minutes on a spin cycle after weight training. You will have stressed the muscles through weight training and the sport-specific task that follows will help to re-coordinate the firing patterns of your muscles. A runner or games player could achieve the same by performing some light strides after a weights workout.
2. Devise a progressive weight-training programme to accompany the demands of your sport, but never lose sight of the sport itself. Weight

training is largely peripheral to performance unless it is adequately channelled into performance.

3. Select exercises, particularly during key training phases, which replicate the movement and have a similar speed element to the sport in question.

4. Take your level of maturity as well as your sport into account when devising your programme of weight training.

5. Do not turn into a gym narcissist, marvelling at your great new physique; it could turn into a burdensome suit of armour for you to haul around.

6. The more experienced the performer, the more the coach will have to work at exploring new avenues for enhancing sports performance. Revisiting a weights programme could be crucial; look closely at the transition to competitive season phases and check out whether previous strength gains really are improving sports performance.

John Shepherd

These medicine ball workouts can do wonders for running velocity and power

The medicine ball has been used as an athletic training aid for decades in Europe, but only in recent years has the value of medicine ball training been recognised in the United States. Many collegiate and professional sports teams are now incorporating this form of strength development into their training, and with proper guidance runners can also benefit from using the medicine ball.

Most medicine ball drills involve lifting, throwing and catching the ball, but the real focal point for such activities is the muscular 'corset' which surrounds the junction between the trunk and the legs. This meeting point, called the 'core' area of the body, is coordinated and held together by the abdominal, spinal erector, hip flexor and gluteal (buttock) muscles. This central region is also called the 'power zone' of the body, because force 'moves' through this area, from one leg to the other during the act of running and also because the core muscles must stabilise the body during foot strike, so that unnecessary motions are minimised and all the power created by the hip and leg muscles can be used to drive the body forward.

Most runners focus on the core area at least to a small extent in their training by carrying out conventional abdominal and low back exercises such as crunches and back extensions. However, during the running motion, the amount of active trunk flexion (carried out by the abdominal muscles) is rather negligible, as is the extent of trunk extension (a function of the low back muscles and gluteals). Compared with direct flexion and extension, there is much more rotational action in the trunk during running, yet most runners totally ignore workouts which would improve the rotational strength of their core muscles.

Medicine ball training, however, can give you additional specific strength, which can be used directly during your workouts and races to improve your running velocity and overall power. The following group of exercises can provide runners competing at all distances with considerably improved core strength. Typical training weights for medicine balls range from two to 15 pounds. Larger balls (up to 25 pounds or so) are used by certain strength athletes (weight lifters, football players, body builders) but are unnecessary for runners. In fact, most runners will do very well with a set of three balls which weigh about two, four, and six pounds (approximately one, two, and three kilograms, respectively).

The exercises

1. The standing trunk twist (hammer twist)

Muscle groups emphasised: Hip and leg muscles, abdominal and oblique muscles and spinal erectors.

Value for runners: This exercise develops dynamic stability strength for all of the core muscles in a standing posture, making the exercise more specific to running than many of the conventional abdominal and low back exercises that are performed in a seated position. Strong core muscles provide for an upright and economical running posture, as well as a strong anchor point for the propulsive muscles in the legs.

Weight of ball: Two pounds for beginners, four to six pounds for advanced athletes.

Other equipment: A towel.

Instructions: Place your towel flat on the ground and then put the medicine ball in the centre of the towel. Bring the ends of the towel, one at a time, over the top of the ball to create a 'ball in a sack' effect. Start the exercise with your feet shoulder-width apart and your weight shifted on to your right foot. Twist your body to the right with your hands grasping the ends of the towel and the ball positioned behind your right shoulder. While keeping your arms straight, swing the ball out away from your body towards the front and then to the left in a wide arc, while bending your legs and 'sitting' into a shallow squat position as the ball reaches the middle of the arc in front of you. Continue this arc until you finish the swing with the weight shifted onto your left foot, with your hands still grasping the ends of the towel and the ball now behind your left shoulder. Immediately swing the ball back to the starting position, and repeat the swinging motion back and forth for a total of 10 to 15 repetitions on each side. Begin this exercise in a slow manner and progress in speed (while still maintaining good control) over a period of several weeks. Perform two to three sets total.

2. Hanging body flex

Muscle groups emphasised: Abdominal, oblique and hip flexor muscles.

Value for runners: This exercise strengthens the integrative action of the muscles, which raise the thighs and stabilise the pelvis. This provides for a powerful knee drive and an economical running posture.

Weight of ball: Two pounds for beginners, four to six pounds for advanced athletes.

Other equipment: A horizontal/chin-up bar.

Instructions: Start from a hanging position with your arms overhead and your legs extended straight down towards the floor. The medicine ball should be placed between your feet and held there firmly by squeezing the feet and legs together. Raise your knees towards your chest (with knees bent) while maintaining a firm grip on the ball with your feet and ankles. Flex your toes and feet up towards your knees throughout the entire movement. Return to the starting position by extending your legs back down towards the ground under control. Perform the movement at a slow speed during the first few sessions and progress to a moderate speed over time. Use 10 to 15 repetitions and two to three sets per workout.

3. Walking trunk twist

Muscle groups emphasised: Hip and leg muscles, abdominals, obliques and spinal erectors.

Value for runners: This exercise develops stability of the core muscles, much like the hammer twist (exercise 1), but the walking twist also incorporates the integrated muscular action required during rhythmic movement. As the right leg moves forward, the trunk twists to the right, following the same oppositional pattern found in running (right leg forward, left arm forward). The added momentum gained by swinging the ball creates increased tension in the stabilising core muscles, thus strengthening them.

Weight of ball: Two pounds for beginners, four to six pounds for advanced athletes.

Other equipment: A towel.

Instructions: Start from a standing position with your feet parallel and the ball secured firmly within the towel and held up behind your right shoulder. Step forward with your left leg and simultaneously swing your arms through a wide arc in front of you. Continue the swing until your arms are shifted to the left and the ball has stopped behind your left shoulder. Continue the exercise by stepping forward with your right leg while simultaneously swinging the ball back behind your right shoulder. The swings should be fairly slow as you learn the exercise but will progress to a moderate (but controlled) speed over time. Repeat the action (stepping and swinging) for a total of 10 to 20 repetitions (five to 10 swings on each side) before resting for a few moments. Repeat for a total of two to three sets.

4. Jump and pick up

Muscle groups emphasised: The hip and leg muscles.

Value for runners: This exercise activates both the extensors and flexors of the hip during the jumping phase of the drill and thus improves explosive leg power for both the push-off and leg-swing or knee-drive portions of the running stride.

Weight of ball: Two pounds for beginners, four to six pounds for advanced athletes.

Training note: To lessen the chance of injury, perform this drill on a resilient surface such as a wood floor, synthetic track, or grass.

Instructions: Start with your feet flat on the ground and the ball held firmly between your ankles. Your knees should be bent slightly so that you are in a shallow squatting position. From this position, perform an explosive jump upward and lift the ball in front of you by pulling both knees up quickly towards your chest to near chest level. Catch the ball with both hands in front of your chest as your feet land on the ground. Squat down and place the ball between your ankles before repeating the action for a total of six to 10 repetitions. Perform two to three sets.

5. Knee throw and lunge

Muscle groups emphasised: Hip flexors and quadriceps are utilised for the throwing action, quadriceps, gluteals, and hamstrings are used for the lunge, and core stabilisers are involved in both the throw and the lunge.

Value for runners: This exercise develops explosive knee lift, eccentric leg strength and coordination. The knee-drive action is followed immediately by an energy-absorbing landing in the lunge position. This combination of throwing and lunging requires both strength and coordination to complete.

Weight of ball: Two pounds for beginners, four to six pounds for advanced athletes.

Instructions: Start in a standing position with your left foot forward and your right foot two to three feet back (standing start position). Your left arm will hang relaxed at your side while your right hand supports the medicine ball on the front upper third of your right thigh. The knee throw takes place as you step forward with your right foot and drive your right knee forward and explosively upward. Essentially, you are releasing the ball with your right hand and 'throwing' the ball forward with your knee. Your motion continues forward until your right foot lands on the ground in front of you, leaving you in a wide lunge position with your trunk held upright. A wall or partner can return the ball to you. Perform 10 to 15 repetitions with the right leg before switching over to the left. Perform two sets with each leg.

6. Squat, throw, fall and chase

Muscle groups emphasised: Leg muscles, abdominals, spinal erectors and shoulders are utilised for the squat and throw actions. Leg, abdominal, chest and shoulder muscles are stressed during the fall and chase movements.

Value to runners: This drill is the most dynamic of the six exercises. The squat and throw actions develop overall power in the muscles of the hips, legs, back and shoulders, muscles which contribute to a strong push off and proper posture during running. The fall action improves coordination and whole body control, as well as upper torso, abdominal and leg strength. Although some runners may laugh at the idea of practising falling, knowing how to fall can prevent injuries during workouts and races. Most runners will fall at some point in their careers, and for runners in more northerly areas, where ice and snow cover the roads during the winter, slipping and falling is rather commonplace. Also, it is important to be able to recover from falls in race situations (remember Mary Slaney's unfortunate tangle with Zola Budd and subsequent tumble during the 1984 Olympic Games?). The chase part of the exercise teaches you to get back on your feet as quickly as possible after a spill and develops strength and coordination in the shoulders, chest, abdominal area, back, hips and legs.

Weight of ball: Four pounds for beginners, six pounds for advanced athletes.

Training note: Perform this drill on grass or other soft surface to minimise impact forces. Allow yourself at least 15 to 20m of space to sprint forward during the chase action.

Instructions: Start by performing a shallow squat with the medicine ball held in front of you at chest level. Explode forward by extending both legs and arms and pushing (throwing) the ball out in front of you at approximately a 45-degree angle. Continue falling forward and catch yourself by driving one knee forward, landing with your body weight on your lead knee, foot and both hands. Rise as quickly as possible and sprint forward until you catch up with the rolling ball. Strive to keep your momentum moving forward throughout each phase of the exercise, never coming to a complete stop at any time. Walk back to the starting point with the ball and repeat the overall exercise for five to 10 repetitions. Perform two sets per workout.

General training guidelines for medicine ball workouts

Medicine ball exercises represent a form of strength training and are typically performed with other strength exercises, when you are relatively fresh and non-fatigued.

Perform all twisting and lifting exercises slowly and deliberately while you are learning the movements. After a few training sessions, the actions may then be speeded up to a moderate speed, but remember to maintain good control at all times.

Focus on developing good form while using light balls early on; progress to heavier balls after three to four weeks.

Core strengthening exercises can actually be carried out frequently (four to six times per week) for relatively brief periods (10 to 15 minutes). The sample programme given below is a guide for including core exercises in your overall training programme (many other programmes are possible).

Monday   Medicine ball exercises 1 and 2 (after a tempo workout)
Tuesday   Traditional core exercises such as abdominal crunches, back extensions, etc (after your usual weight-training routine)
Wednesday Medicine ball exercises 5 and 6 (after your speed work)
Thursday   Break day – no core training
Friday   Traditional core exercises (after long, moderate exertion)
Saturday   Medicine ball exercises 3 and 4 (after weight training)
Sunday   Rest day – no core training

Walt Reynolds

An excellent way to build strength endurance

During the past few years, endurance athletes in a number of sports have added resistance exercises to their training programmes in an effort to boost their muscle power and decrease their risk of injury. Scientific studies have linked resistance training with a reduced rate of injury in athletes. This is probably because resistance work fortifies leg muscles and strengthens 'weak links' in athletes' bodies, including the often-injured hamstrings and shin muscles, as well as abdominal and low back muscles.

Resistance work can also improve tendon and ligament strength and increase bone density, effects that should help to lower injury rates. In addition, resistance workouts heighten body awareness, upgrade coordination, reduce body fat levels and improve self-esteem, all of which can contribute to improved performance during competition.

For athletes, the general preparation period before the beginning of actual competitions is an ideal time to initiate a resistance-training programme. A four to eight-week period of sound resistance training helps to develop a nice foundation of suppleness (mobility), strength, and stamina (endurance), to which athletes can add speed and racing skill just before the competitive season begins.

'Circuit training' is an excellent way to build strength and stamina simultaneously. The circuit training format utilises a group of strength exercises (usually six to 10 or more) that are completed sequentially (one exercise after another). Each exercise is performed for a specified number of repetitions or for a prescribed time period before moving on to the next exercise. The exercises within each circuit are separated by brief, timed rest intervals and each circuit is separated by a longer rest period. The total number of circuits performed during a training session may vary from two to six depending on your training level, your period of training (preparation or competition) and your primary training objective (you may be developing total work capacity, boosting your power, or engaging in 'active rest', for example.)

I have designed this special circuit training with the following objectives in mind:
1. The circuit work will increase your general work capacity by improving your ability to tolerate increasing levels of muscular fatigue (stamina improvement).
2. Over time, the circuit training will have shorter and shorter rest intervals between exercises, thus maintaining elevated heart rates during the circuit workouts and helping you to upgrade your cardio-respiratory capacity (stamina improvement).
3. Circuit efforts will enhance your overall body strength, including the strength and resiliency of muscles, tendons and ligaments, the integrity of your joints, and the strength and density of your supporting bone structures (strength improvement).
4. The circuits will improve your movement skill and body awareness, because you will perform exercises that utilise body weight as the primary form of resistance (skill improvement).
5. The circuit programme will increase your lean muscle mass by a moderate amount and decrease your body fat levels through high levels of energy expenditure (body composition improvement).

The basic training circuit: recommendations

Your basic training circuit can easily be combined with the mobility training described in an earlier module to form a well rounded training session. A full mobility-plus-circuit workout, including warm-up, mobility training, circuit work and a 10-minute cool-down, can be completed in about an hour or less.

Is that too much time for the busy athlete? No. For one thing, you only need to complete the overall workout twice weekly during your base conditioning period. In addition, the payoffs from circuit training are great. Whether you are a cyclist, a race walker, a runner, a rugby player, a swimmer, or a participant in racquet sports, you will improve your strength, mobility and stamina through circuit training. As a result, you will move much more powerfully as you take part in your sport.

Bear in mind, though, that for best results the circuit training sessions should not be performed on consecutive days. If you are carrying out other intensive training on the same day as the circuit work, undertake the intensive work before the circuit training, since fatigue levels from the circuit might well interfere with training intended to develop speed, power, or event specific endurance. Better yet, carry out circuit training on days during which other training is of low intensity. Do not do your circuit training on a rest day, however; rest really means rest.

Here is your sequential format for each circuit:
1. Total body exercise
2. Upper body exercise
3. Lower body exercise
4. Core/trunk exercise
5. Total body exercise
6. Upper body exercise
7. Lower body exercise
8. Core/trunk exercise.

Notice that each part of the body is emphasised twice during each circuit. The amount of rest between exercises and the total rest between circuits is described below.

The basic training circuits: how long to work and rest for each exercise			
Exercise	Moderate circuit (work/rest ratio)	Moderate/hard circuit (work/rest times)	Hard circuit (work/rest)
1. four-count squat thrusts	15 sec:15 sec	20 sec:20 sec	30 sec:30 sec
2. push-ups	15 sec:15 sec	20 sec:20 sec	30 sec:30 sec
3. scissor step-ups	15 sec:15 sec	20 sec:20 sec	30 sec:30 sec
4. abdominal sit-backs	15 sec:15 sec	20 sec:20 sec	30 sec:30 sec
5. squats to presses	15 sec:15 sec	20 sec:20 sec	30 sec:30 sec
6. body weight rows	15 sec:15 sec	20 sec:20 sec	30 sec:30 sec
7. one-leg squats	10 sec for each leg: 20 sec rest	15 sec for each leg: 30 sec rest	20 sec for each leg: 30 sec rest
8. low-back stabilisers	15 sec:15 sec	20 sec:20 sec	30 sec:30 sec
Rest between circuits	2 minutes	2 minutes	3 minutes

Perform the exercises in the order indicated, starting with four-count squat thrusts and then proceeding to push-ups etc. When you finish each circuit by completing the low back stabilisers, rest for the indicated amount of time and then cycle back to the four-count squat thrusts. Note that work/rest times vary for the three different types of circuits – moderate, moderate/hard and hard.

Circuit training progression: making your circuit training more difficult over time			
Week	Circuit type	Number of circuits/workout	Total work (seconds)
1	moderate	2	250
2	moderate/hard	2	340
3	hard	2	500
4	moderate	3	375
5	moderate/hard	3	510
6	moderate/hard	4	680
7	hard	3	750
8	moderate/hard	3	510

The eight exercises in your circuit

For each circuit, do the following exercises:

1. Four-count squat thrusts

- Stand with your arms held at your sides, then squat down, placing both hands in front of you on the floor.
- With arms straight and your weight resting on both hands, quickly extend both legs backward (hop backward), ending in a front support position.
- Return legs forward (hop forward), ending in a low squat position with hands on the floor.
- Finally, jump into the air and return to a standing position. Repeat each of these four steps, in order, to a rhythmic 1-2-3-4 count, without pausing between counts or repetitions.

How will this exercise benefit you?

The high degree of amplitude (joint motion) at your hips and knees, combined with the resistance provided by your body weight, will develop strength and mobility in your knee and hip joints, important for high-speed movement. The front support position develops stability and strength in the upper trunk, abdominal and pelvic regions, strength that is necessary to control torso movements during the running stride or when you strike a ball. The jump added to the exercise as you return to a standing position greatly increases your cardiac demand, hikes the power of your leg muscles and increases the impact forces (upon landing) as well, fortifying the bones in your legs and feet. Use caution, though; perform the movements on a gym floor or grass, not on concrete.

2. Push-ups

- Start in the front support position with your hands and toes on the floor and trunk, hips and legs extended.
- Bend your arms and lower your chest to the floor. Then push your body upward as you straighten your arms, returning to the front support position.
- Repeat this action rhythmically and continuously without stopping for the allotted time.

How does this benefit you?

Push-ups are well known for increasing upper body strength, but their value in developing abdominal and hip flexor stability is often ignored. This improved stability helps to control hip, trunk and shoulder movements as you move quickly and also promotes balance between the upper and lower body.

3. Scissor step-ups

- Use a step or bench which is approximately mid shin to knee height. Put your left foot on the step, with your right foot on the floor and your arms at your sides.
- Then push down with your left leg and drive your body upward rapidly, switching support (hopping) from left foot to right foot as your body reaches its maximal vertical height.
- With your right foot supporting your body, lower the left foot to the floor rapidly but under control.
- Repeat this action continuously, back and forth from foot to foot, without pausing at the top or bottom positions.

How can this help you?

The scissor step-up develops leg strength, power and dynamic balance control (coordination), without which you can not move quickly, whether it is from one end of the football pitch to the other, from the baseline to the net on a tennis court, or from the start to the finish of a 10k race. Cardiovascular benefits of this exercise can be increased by speeding up your stepping cadence or by increasing the height of the step. Step heightening also enhances leg muscle power and improves mobility of the hip and knee joints.

4. Abdominal sit-backs

- For this exercise, use a step, bench, or chair which does not have a vertical support for your back. Sit with your legs bent and your arms extended in front of you, and then recline your trunk backward at the hips by about 45 degrees. That is your starting point for the exercise.
- To do the sit backs, raise both arms simultaneously overhead while maintaining tight abdominal muscles and a straight chest. Then simply return your arms to the extended position in front of you, without moving your trunk or legs.
- Repeat this back and forth arm action in a smooth, continuous fashion without pausing at any point during the movement.

How will this exercise benefit you?

The increased abdominal stability gained from sit backs carries over to improved posture and better core stability as you run. A strong pelvic girdle and trunk provide the anchor point for a strong pair of legs, allowing you to use your legs in a maximally powerful manner during quick sprints or during sustained, vigorous running.

5. Squats to presses

- Use two dumbbells, each weighing approximately 10% of your body weight (*eg* if you weigh 150 pounds, each dumbbell should be 15 pounds).

Individuals with less strength-training experience may start with dumbbells which weigh 5% of body weight, while stronger athletes can use dumbbells checking in at 20% of body weight. You may need to experiment a bit, using a weight that makes the exercise challenging but achievable. If dumbbells are unavailable, a barbell of comparable total weight can be utilised.

- To do the exercise, stand upright with your feet spaced about hip-to shoulder-width apart and your hands supporting the dumbbells in front of your shoulders.
- Squat down until your thighs form an angle of 90 degrees with your shins (a half squat), while maintaining a reasonably upright posture with your torso and while keeping your hands in front of your shoulders.
- Then rise quickly from the squat position while pressing (pushing) the dumbbells overhead simultaneously. Both arms and legs should reach full extension at the same time (you will end up standing tall with legs straight and arms straight overhead).
- Lower the dumbbells in a controlled fashion to the starting position.
- Repeat this three-count movement smoothly and continuously.

How can this help you as an athlete?

Squats to presses increase strength and power in your legs, hips, low back, abdominals, shoulders and arms. The whole body involvement of the squat to press increases your cardio-respiratory requirements, compared to the more commonly used, isolated pressing exercises, such as bench and shoulder presses.

6. Body weight rows

- For this one, you will need a horizontal bar or beam which is sturdy enough to support your body weight. Set the bar at approximately the height of your navel (when you are standing straight up).
- To start the exercise, lie under the bar and grip with both hands at slightly wider than shoulder width. Your heels should be on the floor and your body should be straight and rigid from your shoulders to your ankles.
- Then, with your feet acting as a fulcrum, pull your chest up to the bar by bending your elbows and pulling them backwards.
- Return to the starting position by straightening your arms in a controlled manner and repeat the overall action for the time period specified in the chart.

How can this exercise help you?

The body weight row does for the back-side of the body what the push-up does for the front-side. Body weight rows improve pulling strength of the upper back, shoulder and arm muscles, but they also serve to increase stabilising strength in the low back, gluteals and hamstrings, all of which are critically important for quick movement whenever you participate in your sport. You will achieve a balance between lower and upper body strength by performing this exercise.

7. One-leg squats

- You will need a bench or step six to eight inches in height. Stand with your left foot flat on the floor and your right foot behind you and elevated on the step. The distance between your feet should be approximately the length of your shin, and most of your weight should rest on the heel of your left foot.
- To do the exercise, bend your left knee and lower your body until the left knee makes an angle of 90 degrees between the thigh and lower leg.
- Return to the starting position by straightening your left leg, while maintaining an upright posture with your trunk.
- Repeat this action with the left leg for the specified amount of time, and then switch to the right leg.

How do one-leg squats help you?

This exercise develops muscle strength in the quads, hamstrings and gluteals, the muscles which provide much of your power while running. The actual motion of the one-leg squat closely resembles the 'front side' mechanics of the hip and knee during the actual running stride. By strengthening your hip and knee joints in a coordinated and integrated fashion, your leg strength and running power should improve tremendously. One-leg squats can also help you improve your vertical jumping ability.

8. Low back stabilisers

- For this exercise, you will need a bench, padded table, or 'Roman Chair' bench.
- Lie face down with your body extended and your hips at the edge of the supporting surface of the bench. Your arms should be extended straight down towards the floor in front of you. For added stability, it helps if your feet are wedged between the end of the bench and a wall.
- Smoothly raise both arms over your head simultaneously while maintaining your trunk in full extension (your body should be horizontal to the floor and held straight as an arrow), and then return both arms to the starting position.
- Repeat this action over and over again for the prescribed time period.

How can this exercise benefit you?

Heightened low back strength provides for proper posture while running and also provides excellent 'motion control' of the torso and hips throughout the running stride. As a result, you will move more quickly, whether it is to return a serve on the tennis court or to reach the football in time to score a goal.

Remember that improvements in how your body functions can occur whenever you overload your body's systems. This circuit programme provides an overload of your cardio-respiratory system (especially the hard circuits), taxes your muscular system by forcing it to work against increased resistance, and forces the key joints involved in moving your body to go through a wider range of motion than they commonly encounter. The result, I believe, will be better, more powerful performances.

Walt Reynolds

Jump to it to develop elastic strength

Introduction

Speed and strength are integral components of fitness found in varying degrees in virtually all athletic movements. Simply put, the combination of speed and strength is power. For many years coaches and athletes have sought to improve power in order to enhance performance. Throughout this century, and no doubt long before, jumping, bounding and hopping exercises have been used in various ways to enhance athletic performance. In recent years this distinct method of training for power or explosiveness has been termed plyometrics. Whatever the origins of the word, the term is used to describe the method of training which seeks to enhance the explosive reaction of the individual through powerful muscular contractions as a result of rapid eccentric contractions.

Muscle mechanism

The maximum force that a muscle can develop is attained during a rapid eccentric contraction. However, it should be realised that muscles seldom perform one type of contraction in isolation during athletic movements. When a concentric contraction occurs (muscle shortens) immediately following an eccentric contraction (muscle lengthens) then the force generated can be dramatically increased. If a muscle is stretched, much of the energy required to stretch it is lost as heat, but some of this energy can be stored by the elastic components of the muscle. This stored energy is available to the muscle only during a subsequent contraction. It is important to realise that this energy boost is lost if the eccentric contraction is not followed immediately by a concentric effort. To express this greater force the muscle must contract within the shortest time possible. This whole process is frequently called the stretch shortening cycle and is the underlying mechanism of plyometric training.

Choose the method to fit the sport

The golden rule of any conditioning programme is specificity. This means that the movement you perform in training should match, as closely as possible, the movements encountered during competition. If you are a rugby player practising for the line-out or a volleyball player interested in increasing vertical jump height, then drop jumping or box jumping may be the right exercise. However, if you are a javelin thrower aiming for a more explosive launch, upper-body plyometrics is far more appropriate.

Plyometric exercises

The following are examples of lower-body and upper-body plyometric exercises.

Lower body

Drop jumping: This exercise involves the athlete dropping (not jumping) to the ground from a raised platform or box and then immediately jumping up. The drop down gives the pre-stretch to the leg muscles and the vigorous drive upwards the secondary concentric contraction. The exercise will be more effective the shorter the time the feet are in contact with the ground. The loading in this exercise is governed by the height of the drop, which should be in the region of 30cm to 80cm. Drop jumping is a relatively high-impact form of plyometric training and would normally be introduced after the athlete had become accustomed to lower impact alternatives, such as two footed jumping on the spot.

Bounding and hurdling: If forward motion is more the name of your game, try some bounding. This is a form of plyometric training, where over-sized strides are used in the running action and extra time spent in the air. A two-legged bound reduces the impact to be endured, but to increase the intensity one-legged bounding, or hopping, can be used. Bounding upstairs is a useful way to work on both the vertical and horizontal aspects of the running action. Multiple jumps over a series of obstacles such as hurdles are a valuable drill for athletes training for sprinting or jumping events.

Examples of lower body plyometric exercises with intensity level:

Exercise	Intensity level	Examples
Standing-based jumps (on-the-spot)	Low	Tuck jumps, split jumps
Jumps from standing	Low to medium	Standing long jump, standing hop, standing jump for height
Multiple jumps from standing	Medium	Bounds, bunny-hops, double-footed jumps over low hurdle, double-footed jumps up steps
Multiple jumps with run-in	High	11-stride run + two hops and a jump into a sandpit, two-stride run-in + bounds
Depth jumping	Very high	Jumps down and up off a box (40cm to 100cm) bounding up a hill
Eccentric drop and hold drills	Very high	Hop and hold, bound/hop/bound/hop over 30m (athlete stops and holds on each landing before springing into the next move), drop and hold from a height of 1m

Upper body

A variety of drills can be used to make the upper body more explosive:

Press-ups and hand clap: Press-ups, with a hand clap in between, are a particularly vigorous way to condition the arms and chest. The pre-stretch takes place as the hands arrive back on the ground and the chest sinks, and this is followed quickly by the explosive upward action. Once again, to get the best training effect keep the time in contact with the ground to a minimum.

Medicine ball: Another means of increasing upper body strength popular with throwers is to lie on the ground face-up. A partner then drops a medicine ball down towards the chest of the athlete, who catches the ball (pre-stretch) and immediately throws it back. This is another high-intensity exercise and should only be used after some basic conditioning.

Planning a plyometric session

The choice of exercises within a session and their order should be planned. A session could:
- begin with exercises that are fast, explosive and designed for developing elastic strength (low hurdle jumps, low drop jumps)
- work through exercises that develop concentric strength (standing long jump, high hurdle jumps)
- finish with training for eccentric strength (higher drop jumps).

An alternative session could:
- begin with low hurdle jumps
- progress to bounding and hopping
- continue with steps or box work
- finish with medicine ball workout for abdominals and upper body.

Warm-up

A thorough warm-up is essential prior to plyometric training. Attention should be given to jogging, stretching (static and ballistic), striding and general mobility, especially about the joints involved in the planned plyometric session. A cool-down should follow each session.

How many?

It is wise not to perform too many repetitions in any one session. Since it is a quality session, with the emphasis on speed and power rather than endurance, it's best to split the work into sets with ample recovery in between.

Where to do it and what to wear

For bounding exercises use surfaces such as grass or other resilient surfaces. Avoid cement floors because there is no cushioning. Choose well cushioned shoes that are stable and can absorb some of the inevitable impact. All athletes should undergo general orthopaedic screening before engaging in plyometric training. Particular attention should be given to structural or postural problems that are likely to predispose the athlete to injury.

Conditioning for plyometrics

Higher than normal forces are put on the musculoskeletal system during plyometric exercises so it is important for the athlete to have a good sound base of general strength and endurance. Most experts state that a thorough grounding in weight training is essential before you start plyometrics. It has been suggested that an athlete be able to squat twice their body weight before attempting depth jumps. However, less intensive plyometric exercises can be incorporated into general circuit and weight training during the early stages of training so as to progressively condition the athlete. Simple plyometric drills such as skipping, hopping and bounding should be introduced first. More demanding exercises such as flying-start single-leg hops and depth jumps should be limited to thoroughly conditioned athletes.

Young athletes

Some authors suggest that moderate jumps can be included in the athletic training of very young children (Lohman, 1989). However, great care needs to be exerted when prescribing any training procedures for pre-adolescent children. Because of the relatively immature bone structure in pre-adolescent and adolescent children, the very great forces exerted during intensive depth jumps should be avoided (Smith, 1975).

Summary

Plyometric-type exercises have been used successfully by many athletes as a method of training to enhance power. In order to realise the potential benefits of plyometric training, the stretch shortening cycle must be invoked. This requires careful attention to the technique used during the drill or exercise. The rate of stretch rather than the magnitude of stretch is of primary importance in plyometric training. In addition, the coupling time or ground contact time must be as short as possible.

The challenge to you as coach or athlete is to select or create an exercise that is specific to the event and involves the correct muscular action. As long as you remember to stay specific and to ensure there is a pre-stretch first, the only limit is your imagination. Plyometric exercise and weight training can be combined in complex training sessions to further develop explosive power.

Brian Mackenzie

Jumpers, throwers and sprinters can improve their results by using the Complex system

Traditional strength workouts usually consist of a selection of resistance exercises that target the large and sport-specific muscle groups. Particular training systems can vary, but essentially strength work involves moderate to heavy resistance, 75% to 90% of maximum, with a training volume of three to five sets per exercise. There are two main training effects that come about from this kind of strength routine. The first is an increased neural activation, and this will improve within a few weeks. Increased neural activation means that the maximum amount of muscle fibre recruitment is enhanced, together with the efficiency with which the motor units are activated. All this makes for an increased strength potential. The second training effect is hypertrophy or increased muscle mass. This normally occurs after two to three months of training. Hypertrophy leads to strength improvement because of an increase in the cross-sectional area of the muscle fibres, and thus more force can be exerted when the muscle fibres contract.

The increased strength that results from strength training has been shown to improve sports performance, particularly in terms of sprinting, jumping and throwing, or the speed strength events. However, good as strength training is, one must always remember that it will only go so far in improving speed strength performance. The problem is that the neural activation effects described above are mainly confined to untrained subjects. Once an athlete becomes an experienced lifter, they will benefit from less and less neural activation, particularly in rate-of-force-development (RFD). RFD is simply the speed with which force is achieved during a movement. Thus the greater the RFD, the more explosive and powerful the movement, which is why RFD is crucial for success in speed strength events.

As the neural improvements tail off, any further strength gains from traditional strength work are mostly due to increases in muscle mass. This is not necessarily desirable, because strength gains due to hypertrophy tend to involve high forces at slow speeds, and this is not useful for sports performance. For example, it takes around 400 milliseconds to develop maximum force during a squat exercise, but the foot-ground contact time during sprinting is around 90 milliseconds, so there is not time to produce maximum force during sprint running. Thus, during speed strength events such as sprinting, it is the RFD that becomes more important than absolute strength, so that as much force as possible can be developed in the limited time available.

Supercharging your type IIb fibres

As traditional strength training falls short in developing RFD, there comes a point in an athlete's training when the need to develop maximum strength is replaced by the need to develop power and RFD. When it comes to RFD, the muscle fibres that must be targeted are the type IIb fibres, as these are the ones that produce force most explosively, allowing for maximum power. However, actually training these supercharged type IIbs is harder than you might imagine. Even bodybuilders and power lifters, who do masses of strength work, have highly developed type IIa fibres but are not powerful or explosive because they have not trained their type IIbs.

The sorts of exercise that target the type IIbs are speed strength exercises such as weighted squat jumps, or plyometric exercises such as drop jumps and hops, etc. These exercises involve lower forces than traditional strength work but are performed at much faster speeds, thus targeting the type IIbs. The training effects from these exercises are increased power and RFD. Many athletes include regular plyometric or speed strength workouts in their schedules and are well aware of the benefits. However, it is slightly less well known that the combination of traditional strength with power and/or plyometric exercises together results in even greater type IIb recruitment and consequently greater improvements in power and RFD. Hence the development of a training system that is called Complex training, which is quite simply the combination of weight-training exercises with speed or plyometric exercises within the same workout.

Complex by name, simple by design

The main essence of Complex training is that the content of a training session and the quality to which it is performed are the two important variables, not the volume of weights lifted. By adding explosive exercise to the traditional strength work, Complex training makes the whole session more functional and thus the training adaptations will actually benefit the athlete in terms of sports performance. As an athlete, you need to know that what you do in the gym is going to make a difference on the track, field, pitch or court. Spending months improving your squat and bench press PBs, only to discover that your 100m time is still the same, is not a productive use of your precious training time. However, by using the Complex training system you can be confident that your time in the gym will be time well spent.

Although Complex by name, these workouts are really very simple by design. Complex training is basically a workout comprising matched pairs of exercises, a resistance exercise followed by a plyometric or speed exercise. The main condition is that the pair of exercises must involve the same muscle groups. For example, a pair for the legs could be squats followed by squat jumps, and for the upper body we could match bench press with medicine ball chest pass. The rationale behind these matched pairs is that, in layman's terms, the resistance exercise gets the nervous system firing on all cylinders so that the muscles are at maximum potential to perform the plyometric exercise. In effect, the preceding resistance exercise enables you to recruit more type IIb fibres during the explosive exercise, hence the greater training benefit.

Low- and high-level intensity

A Complex workout can be designed at two levels of intensity. The low level would be performed at the preparation phase of the training cycle and the high level during pre-competition and competition phases. The low-level Complex workout involves a range of weight exercises followed later by some matched plyometric exercises. In contrast, the high-level workout involves super-sets of weight and plyometric pairs. This means the athlete performs the weights exercise, *eg* a set of squats, followed immediately by a set of plyometrics, *eg* hops, whereupon the athlete rests. This super-set would be performed three to four times.

The purpose of the low-intensity Complex workout is that it allows the athlete to train at a relatively high volume, which is what is required in the preparation stage. However, by adding some plyometric work in to the routine, the athlete is not neglecting their type IIb fibres. This kind of workout would also be suitable for beginners and junior athletes.

The resistance levels in the low-intensity workout should be 60% to 75% of 1RM. The volume of the weights exercises should be three to five sets of six to 10 repetitions and the rest periods should be around one minute between sets. There should be a rest period of at least three minutes between the weights exercise and its matched plyometric pairing, but no longer than 10 minutes. A practical way to achieve this is to perform three to five sets of your leg weights exercise, followed by three to five sets of an upper body weights exercise, by which time three to five minutes will have passed and the leg plyometric exercise can be performed. The following table gives a sample low-intensity session that can be used in the preparation period.

Exercise	Sets/repetitions	Rest
Squats	3 x 6-10	1 min
Bench press	3 x 6-10	1 min
Vertical jumps	3 x 10	90 secs
Medicine ball chest pass	3 x 10	90 secs
Dumbbell lunge	3 x 8	1 min
Lat pull-down	3 x 6-10	1 min
Step jumps	3 x 16	90 secs
Medicine ball overhead pass	3 x 10	90 secs
Abdominal crunch	4 x 20	1 min
Glute ham raise	3 x 15	1 min
Medicine ball sit-up and throw	3 x 10	90 secs

On to high quality

The high-quality Complex workout involves a smaller volume but a higher intensity of weights. In this workout the resistance and plyometric exercises are in super-set pairs, which facilitate the recruitment of type IIb fibres. This means the athlete performs the sets of weights exercises and then immediately follows this with the plyometric exercise. During this period of training, the choice of plyometric exercises must be more intense and sports specific, so that maximum power is achieved and the session is as relevant as possible. The resistance levels in the high-intensity workout should be 75% to 90% of 1RM. The volume of the weights exercises should be two to four sets of three to six repetitions and the rest periods should be minimal between matched pairs but three to five minutes between sets. The following table gives an example of a high-quality Complex workout performed in the pre-competition period.

Exercise	Sets/repetitions	Rest
Squats, drop jumps	3 x 5	3-5 mins
	3 x 6	
Barbell step-ups, hops (each leg)	2 x 10	3-5 mins
	2 x 5	
Bench press, plyo press-up	2 x 6	3-5 mins
	2 x 5	
Barbell lunges, box jump	2 x 10	3-5 mins
	2 x 10	
Single-arm row, medicine ball backwards throw	3 x 6	3-5 mins
	3 x 6	

In the competition period the volume should drop even further as the quality of the workout ever increases. For example:

Exercise	Sets/repetitions	Rest
Power cleans (unpaired)	2 x 3	3 mins
Squats, hops (each leg)	2 x 4	5 mins
	2 x 6	
Barbell lunges, speed bounds	2 x 8	5 mins
	2 x 10	

Concentrate on quality

It is very important when performing Complex workouts to make them very tough sessions in terms of quality. To get the best out of them, you need to be physically fresh and mentally motivated. This means no tough aerobic or anaerobic training for at least 48 hours before a Complex session. It also means that you must concentrate and perform the exercises to the best of your ability. Type IIb fibres are not magically recruited just by doing a particular training routine; it is up to you to focus and perform the exercises as explosively as possible. The structure of the Complex training session provides an advantage, but this will not be capitalised on unless you push it. To ensure this quality is maintained, you must observe the correct rest periods. A further practical tip to bear in mind is that once the training has started no static stretching exercise should take place, because this will relax the muscles and reduce force production potential. In fact, it is arguable that no static stretching at all should take place in the warm-up for the same reason. Light aerobic activity and active mobility exercise combined with suitable warm-up lifts are more effective.

To sum up, strength training is great, but ultimately it is not the best way to improve performance. Instead, plyometric and speed strength exercises must be included in the training routine. The Complex training system provides a way of combining the two training methods to enhance the training benefit in power and RFD. The Complex workout should follow the usual periodisation cycle, with high-volume, low-intensity and general workouts gradually being replaced by low-volume, high-intensity and specific training.

A brief neuromuscular explanation

The most effective speed strength performance depends on the RFD, the quickness with which force can be achieved during a particular movement. For a rapid RFD, an athlete must recruit their type IIb fibres. These fibres are packaged together in motor units. A motor unit comprises a single motor neuron that is connected to a large number, about 1,000, of these type IIb fibres. It is the motor neuron that switches on the fibres in the motor unit, where one single neuron innervates many fibres. Other types of motor units comprise neurons connected to type IIa fibres and neurons connected to type I (slow-twitch) fibres; however, in these motor units the motor neurons generally connect to fewer muscle fibres. Because of their larger size, the type IIb motor units have a high excitation threshold, which means they are more difficult to turn on, or recruit, than the smaller slow-twitch motor units. This means that to utilise your type IIb fibres you need a maximum level of activation of the corresponding motor neuron for the IIb muscle fibres to be switched on.

It has been shown that after a very high-intensity voluntary contraction, the level of excitation in the motor unit is increased, and this increased excitation can last for several minutes. This is termed a 'post tetanic potentiation' and essentially means that a better recruitment output is achieved for the same neural input. Or, to put it simply, more fast-twitch fibre recruitment for the same voluntary effort.

This has been shown experimentally by H-reflex studies. The H-reflex is the amount of EMG activity innervated by an electric shock. After muscle stimulation, the H-reflex is shown to have increased; thus more muscle fibres have been recruited for the same level of activation. It is this effect that we are capitalising on during Complex training. The weights exercises provide the initial stimulus for the muscles, exciting the nervous system and allowing more muscle recruitment. In particular, more type IIb recruitment, which as we have seen is more difficult. Then, when the plyometric exercise is performed, more type IIb fibres can be recruited and thus more training benefits are achieved. This is why studies have shown that Complex training brings about greater RFD improvement than plyometric training alone.

Raphael Brandon

Module 6

Speed and agility

Introduction

Speed and agility are important attributes in many sports, but often in very different ways, each sport having its own particular demands. For instance (as noted in an earlier module) fencing requires very quick footwork and acceleration but all movements are linear – forwards and backwards. In contrast, racquet sports are multidirectional, with as much lateral movement as linear.

In addition, different sports have different speed profiles. Racquet sports require very fast off-the-mark acceleration, but maximum speed over a longer sprint (30m to 60m) is less important. Rugby and football require both good acceleration and maximum speed. Therefore maximum speed and acceleration need to be differentiated in training.

Overview of the speed and agility module

In this module we look at how you can develop your speed and agility to meet the demands of your sport.
- Brian Mackenzie provides an overview of the principles of speed.
- John Shepherd explains how you develop your speed on a treadmill.
- Alun Williams and Mick Wilkinson explain how tapering can improve your speed.
- Joe Dunbar provides an overview of the energy systems and explains how you can develop your anaerobic capacity (speed).

The articles in this module are applicable to most sports.

Principles of speed training

Speed is the quickness of movement of a limb, whether this is the legs of a runner or the arm of the shot-putter. Speed is an integral part of every sport and can be expressed as any one of, or combination of, the following:

- maximum speed
- elastic strength (power)
- speed endurance.

Speed is influenced by the athlete's mobility, special strength, strength endurance and technique.

Energy system for speed

The anaerobic-alactic pathway supplies energy for absolute speed. The anaerobic (without oxygen) alactic (without lactate) energy system is best challenged as an athlete approaches top speed between 30m and 60m while running at 95% to 100% of maximum. This speed component of anaerobic metabolism lasts for approximately six seconds and should be trained when no muscle fatigue is present (usually after 24 to 36 hours of rest).

How do we develop speed?

The technique of sprinting must be rehearsed at slow speeds and then transferred to runs at maximum speed. The stimulation, excitation and correct firing order of the motor units, each composed of a motor nerve (neuron) and the group of muscles that it supplies, makes it possible for high-frequency movements to occur. The whole process is not totally clear but the complex coordination and timing of the motor units and muscles most certainly must be rehearsed at high speeds to implant the correct patterns.

Flexibility and a correct warm-up will affect stride length and frequency (strike rate). Stride length can be improved by developing muscular strength, power, strength endurance and running technique. The development of speed is highly specific and to achieve it we should ensure that:

- flexibility is developed and maintained all year round
- strength and speed are developed in parallel
- skill development (technique) is pre-learned, rehearsed and perfected before it is done at high speed levels
- speed training is performed by using high velocity for brief intervals. This will ultimately bring into play the correct neuromuscular pathways and energy sources.

When should speed work be conducted?

It is important to remember that the improvement of running speed is a complex process, which is controlled by the brain and nervous system. In order for a runner to move more quickly, the leg muscles of course have to contract more quickly, but the brain and nervous systems also have to learn to control these faster movements efficiently. If you maintain some form of speed training throughout the year, your muscles and nervous system do not lose the feel of moving fast and the brain will not have to re-learn the proper control patterns at a later date.

In the training week, speed work should be carried out after a period of rest or light training. In a training session, speed work should be conducted after the warm-up and any other training should be of a low intensity.

Speed workouts

The following are examples of speed work sessions for a variety of running events:

Event	Speed session
100m	10 x 30m at race-pace from blocks with full recovery 3-4 x 80m at race-pace with full recovery
800m	5 x 200m at goal race-pace with 10 seconds' recovery 4 x 400m at 2-3 seconds faster than current race-pace with two minutes' recovery
1500m	4 x 400m at goal race-pace with 15-10 seconds' recovery 4-5 x 800m at 5-6 seconds per 800m faster than goal race-pace with six minutes' recovery
5000m	4-5 x 800m at four seconds per 800m faster than goal race-pace with 60 seconds' recovery Three x one mile at six seconds per mile faster than goal race-pace with two minutes' recovery
10,000m	3 x 2000m at three seconds per 200m faster than goal race-pace with two minutes' recovery Five x five-minute intervals at current 5k race-pace with three minutes' recovery
Marathon	Six one-mile repeats at 15 seconds per mile faster than goal race-pace with one minute recovery 3 x 3000m at 10k race-pace with six minutes' recovery

Effective methods to develop acceleration:
- All maximum leg strength exercises improve acceleration, as do leg plyometric exercises. Particularly useful ones are standing long jump, standing triple jump, hurdle hops and combination jumps (horizontal).
- Sprint starts. For example, 20 x 5m with 30 seconds' recovery. These can be made more specific by incorporating reactions to signals (eg the ball) or starting from various positions (eg the floor).
- Foot speed drills. For instance, Frappier drills, complete maximum number of foot contacts in 10 seconds.
- Resisted accelerations. Athlete performs maximum 10m efforts with trainer pulling with tubing.

Always finish a workout with normal accelerations

Sprinting speed

Sprinting speed can be developed in a number of ways:

- **Towing** – the athlete is towed behind a motorcycle at a speed of 0.1 to 0.3 seconds faster than the athlete's best for a rolling 30m. This pace is held for 20m to 30m following a gradual build-up to maximum speed over 60m to 70m.
- **Elastic pull** – two tubular elastic ropes are attached to the athlete – two coaches, positioned forward and to each side of the athlete, extend the elastic to full stretch and the athlete is virtually catapulted over the first 10m from a standing or crouched start.

I am sure you can appreciate the potential dangers with these two methods.

Downhill sprinting is a safer alternative for developing sprinting speed. A hill with a maximum of a 15-degree decline is most suitable. Use 40m to 60m to build up to full speed and then maintain the speed for a further 30m. A session could be comprised of two to three sets of three to six repetitions. The difficulty with this method is to find a suitable hill with a safe surface.

Over-speed work could be carried out on the track when there are prevailing strong winds – run with the wind behind you. Athletes must always be completely fresh for speed training if it is to be effective. Therefore no heavy weight training or hard endurance training should be done the day before.

Speed training sessions must always include long rest periods and focus solely on quality. Speed development is about teaching the neuromuscular system to operate at full speed and power and this is not possible if there is any fatigue. If rests are too short, the training will only develop speed endurance and not maximum speed.

Speed reaction drill

The athletes start in a variety of different positions – lying face down, lying on their backs, in a push-up or sit-up position, kneeling or seated. The coach, standing some 30m from the group, then gives a signal for everyone to jump up and run towards the coach at slightly faster than race-pace. Repeat using various starting positions and with the coach standing in different places so that the athletes have to change directions quickly once they begin to run. Speed reaction drills can also be conducted while controlling an item (*eg* football, basketball, hockey ball) with an implement (*eg* feet, hands, hockey stick).

Speed principles

The general principles for improved speed are as follows:

- Choose a reasonable goal for your event and then work on running at velocities which are actually faster than your goal over short work intervals.
- Train at goal pace in order to enhance your neuromuscular coordination,

confidence and stamina at your desired speed.

- At first, utilise long recoveries, but as you get fitter and faster shorten the recovery periods between work intervals to make your training more specific and realistic to racing. Also move on to longer work intervals, as you are able.
- Work on your aerobic capacity and lactate threshold. Conduct some easy-pace runs to burn calories and permit recovery from the speed sessions.
- Work on your mobility to develop a range of movement (range of motion at your hips will affect speed) and assist in the prevention of injury.

Seven-step model

The following is a seven-step model for developing playing speed.

1. Basic training to develop all qualities of movement to a level that will provide a solid base on which to build each successive step. This includes programmes to increase body control, strength, muscle endurance and sustained effort (muscular and cardiovascular, anaerobic and aerobic).
2. Functional strength and explosive movements against medium to heavy resistance. Maximum power is trained by working in an intensity range of 55% to 85% of your maximum intensity (1RM).
3. Ballistics to develop high-speed sending and receiving movements.
4. Plyometrics to develop explosive hopping, jumping, bounding, hitting and kicking.
5. Sprinting form and speed endurance to develop sprinting technique and improving the length of time you are able to maintain your speed.
6. Sport loading to develop specific speed. The intensity is 85% to 100% of maximum speed.
7. Over-speed training. This involves systematic application of sporting speed that exceeds maximum speed by 5% to 10% through the use of various over-speed training techniques.

Brian Mackenzie

How the Frappier super treadmill helps athletes run faster

Getting from A to B in the fastest possible time is the key to performance for most sports, whether you aim to run a marathon in just over two hours or go 'sub-10' for the 100m. Not surprisingly, improving an athlete's speed is a highly valued training objective. This goal has been subject to much research, analysis and systematic treatment, and theories abound as to how it can be achieved. This article focuses on one particular speed development programme, known as the 'Frappier system'. This method adopts a highly systematic approach to speed, with protocols for sprinters, games players and endurance athletes.

American John Frappier began developing his system in the 1980s. After gaining an MSc in sports science, he spent considerable time in Russia with the US junior gymnastics team, where he gained valuable insights into how the former Soviets trained for speed and power. (The Russians were probably the first nation to fully appreciate the benefits of plyometric exercises.) On his return to the States he started working with top NFL (American football) players and began to put together his thoughts on speed development. The first Frappier Acceleration Center opened in 1986 and there are now more than 100 such centres, mostly in the United States.

The system has put through its paces well over 100,000 amateur and professional athletes, the latter group including former tennis ace Steffi Graf, former 400m world record-holder Butch Reynolds, current top Kenyan middle-distance athletes, and numerous internationals and Olympians from an array of sports. The system now has an accredited UK centre in Chiswick (Sport Dimensions), run by Mike Antoniades and Ulick Tarabanov. Since opening the centre in the spring of 2001, they have worked with such notable performers as Chelsea and Bayern Munich footballers and England rugby players.

All athletes, whatever their sport, are put through a six-week 'level one' programme. This is personalised to the strengths and weaknesses of the individual and acts as a gentle introduction to the protocols and techniques of the programme, in particular the use of the 'super treadmill'. Progressions are strictly adhered to and strengths and weaknesses identified in order to ensure safe progression from one level to another. For those seeking absolute speed there are 12 levels to work through, while those after endurance progress through six levels. Both programmes utilise eight-week training cycles.

The 30mph-top-speed treadmill is the key aspect of the Frappier system, although specialised plyometric and weights drills also play a crucial role. It can take time to get to grips with running on the machine, but the combination of inclined/declined running potential (max 40% up, 10% down) increasing belt speed (max 50mph) and an emphasis on biomechanically correct sprinting form is geared to make you a faster athlete.

The Frappier system, just like any other systematic training programme, is based on the overload principle. It relies on the fact that the body will respond to speed overload in the same way it does to progressive resistance or endurance training stimuli – by developing an appropriate physiological response. For speed this means more powerful muscles and an increase in the relevant neuromuscular patterning that will enable an athlete to move faster. Butch Reynolds apparently recorded a speed of 28mph on the treadmill, which is way above the 23mph recorded by Maurice Green during his world-record run.

In technical terms, it is explained that incline running on the treadmill allows for the specific development of the key factors associated with acceleration. In terms of the running action, increased speed can only be accrued from a certain point in the running action. That is from the 'toe off' as the body shifts forwards over the grounded foot and extension occurs through the ankle to the hip. The incline permits the athlete to learn and maintain optimum knee drive, pelvic and trunk positioning and a dorsiflexed or cocked foot strike. Athletes are often filmed on the treadmill for specific technical analysis.

Sprint athletes used to be implored to run on their toes. On reflection, many coaches were probably really asking their athletes to run from a 'high hips' position, trying to prevent them from 'sitting' on each stride and thus denting forward momentum. But if this advice was taken literally, as it was and still is by many, it actually led to the athlete attempting tip-toed sprinting. This is detrimental to speed generation because a breaking effect is caused on each foot strike, as the ankle inevitably yields from its extended position, irrespective of lower limb strength. The dorsiflexed foot position minimises force-absorption and maximises force-return and is recommended not just by Frappier trainers but also by many other top coaches.

How progressive treadmill training boosts speed capability

Readers may be questioning the use of a treadmill in the Frappier system. Here is how UK Frappier coach Antoniades justifies it:

'Our high-speed treadmill allows for specific neuromuscular recruitment and synaptic response. What people do not realise until they run on the treadmill is that it is manufactured to make it as close to running on a track as possible.'

In a recent issue of *Peak Performance,* US editor Owen Anderson questioned the use of such a machine in an athlete's training programme, arguing that foot strike time was increased. He wrote:

'Basically the athletes were trying to create more stability for themselves on the unstable fast moving and/or inclined treadmill by keeping their feet on the belt a little longer than usual.' The Frappier response is that progressive treadmill training allows athletes to achieve greater than 'normal' running speeds – *ie,* those achieved through track work. This, when coupled with the other exercises and drills in the system, is said to lead to optimisation of speed capability.

This belief involves a re-working of the over-speed principle, of which downhill sprinting and sprinting using elastic cords are other examples. These methods and the Frappier super treadmill permit athletes to run at higher than normal speeds. Because of this, their neuromuscular systems adapt to the stimuli of artificially enhanced greater limb speed capability, with the end result that these patterns are 'learned' and the athletes become faster. Away from the treadmill, speed theory has it that the extent of the assistance should not be greater than 4% of an athlete's normal non-assisted top speed, otherwise the stimulus (the decline or the elastic) does the work and not the athlete. The athlete needs to be able to 'fire' their limbs to generate power, not be 'dragged' to super-speed. It is because of this that the other speed enhancement methods are eschewed by the Frappier system. Antoniades explains that the downhill and elastic cord methods are harder to quantify and control than treadmill running, which offers control, regulation and incremental progression.

It is also important to point out that Frappier athletes are encouraged to continue with their normal sport-specific training. At the time I saw the Frappier system in action, Olympic bobsleigher Colin Bryce was being put through his paces while still involved in team training. The system certainly worked for him, as the former strong man became fast enough to push the two-man bob in Salt Lake in 2002.

Beyond the treadmill

What are the other aspects of the Frappier system and how do they contribute to greater speed development? Specialised weights and plyometric exercises have been constructed to complement the treadmill work. The 'pro-implosion' is a sprint arm action mimicking machine, which is also capable of 10 other moves. A dynamic and powerful arm drive is crucial to absolute sprint speed and this machine conditions the upper body accordingly. The 'plyo-press' is a squat/leg press machine which enables the upper thighs to be loaded dynamically in a way that could not happen with free weights. Basically, athletes push themselves dynamically off the machine's platform (as if jumping) and then drive into the next lift/jump (as if performing a plyometric drill). This exercise is performed in a reclined position, with the option of increased resistance from the machine.

I myself had experience of a similar, if more rudimentary, system when competing in the former Czechoslovakia more than 15 years ago. This involved something like a child's swing. You simply plucked up courage, swung towards a wall and used your legs to push yourself dynamically backwards to invoke a plyometric response. Frappier obviously took some of these former Eastern Bloc conditioning ideas and refined them for use in his own system.

The Frappier system also offers a rehabilitation programme. 'This is particularly unique in the UK, as we get athletes or individuals back to fitness and competitive sport much more quickly and safely,' explained Antoniades. The system has demonstrated particular success with knee and back problems and, although rehabilitation is beyond the scope of this article, it does appear that miraculous recoveries are possible. Antoniades gave the example of Chelsea player Jesper Groenjaer, who had knee ligament surgery in September 2001. In February 2002 he was put through the Frappier system, while still in pain, only able to run at 70% (8mph) and with a big (35%) strength differential between his left and right leg. 'We got Jesper fit in two weeks,' enthused Antoniades. 'That was 12 sessions and he has been playing regularly in

Chelsea's first team ever since.'

The Frappier system does seem to offer real potential for speed enhancement, having taken speed and power development theory from around the world and quantified it into a systematic methodology. Speed is a unique conditioning aspect. It depends on eliciting a very specific physiological response, one that can actually be hindered if the wrong training is performed. The Frappier system seems to have successfully put into one box the right equipment that an athlete needs to get faster.

John Shepherd

Why tapering after intense training boosts sprinting speed

What makes a winning sprinter? The answer to this apparently simple question is a complex one including such elements as mental approach, diet and even clothing. But since sprinting performance is heavily dependent on speed of limb movement, one of the biggest single factors contributing to success is physiology[1]. The muscle fibres in the winning sprinter's legs are able to contract faster over the short period of the sprint than those of their less successful counterparts. Recent research findings have improved our knowledge of how human muscle adapts to training, and the extent to which muscle can alter its ability to meet the fast movement velocities demanded by sprinting performance.

A muscle consists of a bundle of cells known as fibres, bound together by envelopes of a connective tissue called collagen. A single fibre comprises a membrane, many nuclei containing genetic information, and thousands of inner strands running the length of the fibre, called myofibrils. Muscle force production is accomplished through the interaction of two protein filaments that make up the myofibril, actin and myosin.

One component of the myosin filament, known as the myosin heavy chain (MHC), determines the functional abilities of the entire muscle fibre. This heavy chain exists in three forms: I, IIa and IIb. Type I fibres contain a predominance of type I MHC and are commonly called slow-twitch, while fibre types IIa and IIb contain a predominance of type IIa and IIb MHC respectively, and are known as fast-twitch. Slow-twitch fibres are so-called because the maximum contraction velocity of a single fibre is approximately one tenth that of a type IIb fibre[2]. Type I fibres also produce less maximum force than type IIb fibres[3]. Type IIa fibres lie somewhere between type I and type IIb in their maximum contraction velocity and maximum force production.

Because of the high velocity of contraction and the large forces they produce, type IIb fibres are probably one of the key elements required for successful performances in speed-dependent pursuits like sprinting. It is therefore not surprising to find that successful sprint athletes possess more of these IIb fibres than the average person[4]. But is this part of a sprinter's make up pre-determined by genetics? Or can the proportion of type IIb fibres in muscle be increased through training?

Training effects on fibre type

Virtually all the available evidence suggests that the answer to the last question is no. In fact, it has been suggested that type IIb MHC and therefore IIb fibres constitute a 'default' fibre type setting in humans when activity is absent, and evidence of high proportions of this fibre type in paralysed muscle supports this theory[5]. It has also been known for some time that increases in activities like strength or power training can lead to conversion of muscle fibres. But, unfortunately, this conversion operates in one direction only, changing fast type IIb fibres into slower type IIa fibres[6]. Moreover, if heavy loading of muscles continues for a month or more, virtually all type IIb fibres will transform to type IIa, with obvious consequences for sprinting potential[7].

What happens when heavy strength training stops? Do the newly formed type IIa fibres revert to type IIb? The answer is yes, but recent research has revealed some extraordinary results to which a simple yes does not do justice.

Scientists from the Copenhagen Muscle Research Centre examined training and detraining effects on muscle fibre type distribution[8]. Biopsies (muscle samples) were taken from the vastus lateralis muscle of nine young sedentary males. All the subjects then undertook three months of heavy resistance training, aimed predominantly at the quadriceps muscle group, which ended with a second muscle biopsy. The subjects then abruptly ceased training and returned to their normal sedentary lifestyles before providing a third biopsy three months later.

Biopsies from the vastus lateralis were analysed for muscle fibre type distribution and number. As was expected, there was a decrease in the proportion of fast-twitch IIb fibres (from around 9% to 2%) during the resistance-training period. The researchers expected that the proportion of IIb fibres would simply be restored to pre-training values during the detraining period. However, they found to their surprise that the proportion actually doubled to around 18% after three months of sedentary living!

How heavy training followed by tapering produces 'overshoot'

So it seems that a pattern of heavy resistance training followed by decreased activity causes first a decrease then an overshoot in the proportion of the fastest fibre type in the trained/detrained muscle group. An explanation for this overshoot currently eludes researchers, but the findings accord with the theory that muscle fibres 'default' to type IIb with a (relatively) decreased level of activity[5].

Further research using trained athletes as subjects would add weight to these findings. But until then, sprinters may draw the following conclusions: a large increase in training volume for approximately three months will decrease the proportion of IIb fibres in the trained muscles; a subsequent reduction (not cessation) in training volume relative to the heavy resistance training phase should not only reverse this decrease but lead to a significant overshoot in the proportion of IIb fibres. In consequence, the potential for the rapid and forceful muscle contractions so crucial to sprint performance should be enhanced.

This conclusion is in line with the current training practices of many sprint athletes. In the lead-up to the competitive season a heavy resistance training phase is followed by a taper in training volume and intensity[9]. On the evidence of the Copenhagen research, others would be advised to follow their example, with three months of heavy resistance training followed by three months of relative detraining, with relatively reduced training volume in the run-up to key targeted events.

However, as is usually the case, new research findings will probably refine these recommendations over the coming years.

Alun Williams and Mick Wilkinson

References

1. *New Studies in Athletics*, 10 (1), pp29-49
2. *Journal of Physiology*, 472, pp595-614
3. *Journal of Physiology*, 495, pp573-586
4. *Journal of Applied Physiology*, 59, p1716
5. Pflugers Archiv. *European Journal of Physiology*, 431, pp513-518
6. *Journal of Applied Physiology*, 74, pp911-915
7. *Acta Physiologica Scandinavica*, 151, pp135-142
8. *Muscle and Nerve*, 23, pp1095-1104
9. *Medicine and Science in Sports and Exercise*, 27 (8), pp1203-1209.

Take up the anaerobic challenge

Come April, hundreds of runners are digging around at the back of the wardrobe, trying to find that old pair of track spikes. A quick dust to get rid of the cobwebs and it's off to the track, adrenaline pumping because the time has come already for the first track workout of the summer. The county champs are only a month or so away and you are thinking that you have got to get some speed in the legs before the serious stuff gets under way.

But how often do you seriously think about why you are going to the track, what workout you are going to do, and exactly how it is going to help you reach that peak performance on the track, when it counts? Most people tend to gather at the track and do the group session without even stopping to think what the training effect is doing to their body, or how they are going to progress next week, or the week after.

To be sure of what the session is for, how to structure the session in terms of duration and recovery and how the session may fit into your overall programme, it is important to understand energy systems – how the body makes energy available for exercise – especially when running close to your maximum.

The exercising body has three major sources of adenosine triphosphate (ATP), which is the basic unit the body uses to produce energy in working muscles. Two of these are short-term and do not immediately require oxygen, while the other is more long-term, but does require the availability of oxygen. Therefore, the first two are described as 'anaerobic', while the third, the oxidative pathway, is classed as 'aerobic'.

The anaerobic pathways can be further subdivided into the high-energy phosphagen system and the glycolytic pathway. These two short-term energy systems can produce a lot of energy very quickly, but also fatigue rapidly. For example, the high-energy phosphagen system can produce energy at up to three times the rate of the aerobic oxidative system, but fatigues within a number of seconds. This system uses either ATP stored within the muscle or creatine phosphate, which can help produce more ATP via chemical reactions. After a sprint, this system can be repleted, which takes place quickly at first (the first 50% is repleted within 20 or so seconds) and then more slowly (the second 50% takes about 170 seconds). This has important consequences for training programmes.

At a high intensity, the glycolytic pathway can supply energy to the muscles, but again the time-span is limited. If the oxidative system simply cannot supply enough oxygen to cope with the demands of the workload encountered, lactate will start to accumulate in the muscle tissue, which soon diffuses into the blood. If the lactate accumulation is great, the ability to contract the muscle will be inhibited, and there will also be a feeling of pain for the runner.

Recent research studied the muscle metabolism of subjects running a flat-out 400m (*Medicine and Science in Sports and Exercise*, April 1991). It was seen that after 100m, creatine phosphate decreased from 15.8 to 8.3mmol/kg, while peak muscle and blood lactate was 3.6 and 4.7mmol/kg. The rate of muscle and blood lactate was seen to have reached maximum between 200m and 300m. Running speed dropped significantly in the second half of the 400m and the end level of creatine phosphate had fallen to 1.7mmol/kg, while the muscle and blood lactate had shot up to 17.3 and 14.9mmol/kg. The study suggests that the acceleration phase tends to rely on the breakdown of creatine phosphate to produce energy, while the lactate levels start to reach a 'detrimental' point after 300m and lead to a decrease in running speed.

Putting it into practice

Where does all this fit into my training, you may well be asking? If you are a middle-distance runner, you need a great deal of speed, especially in the 800m event and the ability to run fast, be it from the gun or at the end of the race. If you are thinking this does not apply to you because you run the 10,000m or the marathon, think again. Remember how fast the last lap of the 10,000m was in the last major games that you watched; remember how Douglas Wakiihuri easily dealt with Steve Moneghetti in the London Marathon in 1989. Whatever the event, right down to a Southern League 5000m, it seems almost inevitable that you are going to need an element of speed.

The most critical distinction to make in planning your anaerobic training is deciding whether you are about to do a session to train your high-energy phosphagen system, or train for pure speed, or work on the anaerobic endurance or speed endurance aspect. Both need to be worked on if you are to be fully prepared when you reach the start line, but they will need quite different sessions.

Think for a minute about why you do intervals. For the aerobic system, they are useful because, according to American physiologist David Lamb, they can increase your maximal aerobic capacity, help you to perform at a high percentage of your VO_2max, and increase the distance that you can run fuelled by a set amount of oxygen (*ie*, your running economy is improved). With intervals, you can perform a greater overall volume of work than in the steady state, albeit with rest in between. These are preferred in anaerobic training, but by manipulating the work-to-rest ratio you can control what energy pathway you are going to train in your session.

If you are going to train your body for speed, you need to work in short bouts, with lots of recovery. This means that to avoid accumulating large amounts of lactate, the sprint should be of about 10 seconds' duration, and the recovery should be up to three minutes because it takes about 190 seconds for ATP and creatine phosphate to be repleted in the muscle. So, although you may be a distance runner, if you are to train this system effectively, you have to train like a sprinter. The work periods are hard but you should get to like the more leisurely recovery.

The shape of your session

How do I progress with such a session, you are probably asking? You do not want to increase the duration of the repetitions, otherwise you are starting to train a different pathway, so try to improve the quality of the sprints; that is, run quicker. This should happen over a series of weeks with practice, as the body becomes more coordinated and the neuromuscular ability is improved. Your pure speed session may look something like:

- five x 60m to 80m with three minutes' recovery between sets.

This can then progress to three sets of sessions, with about six to eight minutes between sets. The recovery can be reduced very gradually, as the rate of repletion is improved with the training. Therefore, the recovery between sets can be chopped first to, say, four or five minutes, followed through the weeks by slicing 10 seconds off the rest between repetitions. There is no evidence that the total amount of ATP or creatine phosphate increases in the muscle through repeated weeks of training, but the recovery rate should improve, as should the quality of work, which is the aim of the actual session anyway.

In deciding what sort of intensity to run at, remember that this is a quality session when you should be at maximal speed, so heart rate is not a good indicator at such intensities. The session should be used most in the pre-season period, so once or twice a week in April and May would be the recommendation and once a week for maintenance once the season is under way.

In building anaerobic endurance, the session needs to be of sufficient intensity to challenge the lactate system, yet not so fast that extreme tiredness is encountered and the session is ruined. Here there are far more options and many top runners train in different manners. There is a case for doing what suits and works for the individual, but certain principles still apply.

For middle-distance runners, the suggested total volume of the session may be two to three times the competition distance, but this will depend upon the quality of the session. If the intervals are run quickly, you will not be able to run many, despite ample recovery, yet if the repetitions are a few seconds slower, far more will be endured. It is common to start off the pre-competition with a series of steadier repetitions, building on the endurance gained over the winter and speed up as the season progresses. This means that the session for a two-minute 800m runner may be:
  • 10 x 200m in 30 seconds (with 60 seconds' recovery).

As the season progresses the speed of the repetitions can increase, which will be allowed for by more recovery. This means a month later the session for the same athlete may be:
  • four x 200m in 26/27 seconds (with two minutes' recovery).

As competition gets closer the athlete will be in a better position to handle longer anaerobic repetitions, with good recovery, so the same athlete may attempt:
  • two x 400m in 54/ 55 seconds (with about 10 minutes' recovery).

In all three cases, the glycolytic pathway will have been challenged and large levels of lactate will have accumulated by the end of the session. However, the athlete will be in a better position to handle the race condition by completing the third session, as this is a bit more specific to the demands of 800m.

Another idea is to practise running repetitions with a decreasing recovery during the session. Here the athlete gets used to trying to maintain pace under greater conditions of fatigue. The athlete may be performing repetitions of 300m, as this was seen earlier to be the distance where the accumulation of lactate peaks. You would choose this type of session in order to train your body for lactate tolerance. This sort of session would also take place during the pre-competitive season, or in the early competitive phase. Such a session might be:

- five x 300m with a recovery of 3, 2.5, 2 and 1.5 minutes.

The pace would be dictated by your ability; the aim would be to run at near-race-pace throughout the session; you are not trying to run faster, as in the previous case. To get the same type of effect again – that is, being able to run fast in a state of tiredness – the 1984 Olympic gold medallist Joaquim Cruz used a session in the competitive season of two sets of:

- one x 600m (1:18) jog 200m, one x 400m (51/52) jog 200m, one x 200m (23/24).

There were three minutes in between sets. Training at such a blistering pace is essential for anyone running 800m in 1:42, but the session could be mimicked with more realistic splits by any 800m runner. The session trains speed endurance, with a picking-up of the pace as you progress.

Some of the Kenyan 5000m runners have been seen to do similar types of sessions in terms of metabolic demand (*ie*, lactate tolerance) but structured in a different manner. One such session is:

- 10 x 400m with five minutes' recovery.

The times for these repetitions for the faster 5000m runners (under 13:30) were a staggering 54/55 seconds, but it should be remembered that this was near the middle of summer, where they wanted to maintain a fast pace. That is why the relatively long recovery of five minutes was allowed. 1500m runners in this country use a similar session of 10 x 400m, but they would use a shorter recovery and a steadier pace, so not training the same energy pathway. Steve Cram has been seen to do such a session in the pre-competitive phase, where he will run the repetitions around four-minute-mile pace (60 seconds a lap) off a minute recovery. Such a session, however, is greatly challenging to the aerobic system as well as the anaerobic system, making it more relevant to the end of the preparation period.

The right session for the right phase

The key to anaerobic training is performing the correct sessions at the right phase of the year. By the time the track season starts, the bulk of the work must have been completed. The only track sessions you need will be maintenance sessions, which consist of a few fast repetitions, with a long recovery, like the two x 400m sessions for the 800m runner. If you run 5000m, why not try something like the Kenyan session in more realistic splits, but with the same type of recovery? A 1500m runner might try:

- three x 600m with seven to eight minutes' slow jog recovery.

The pace will depend on the ability again, but the recovery is chosen because in the trained athlete the lactate clearance should take about seven minutes, with slow jogging. This means that you will not be starting the next repetition with an already high lactate level, and the quality of the session should be maintained. Commonly quoted sessions of Seb Coe are:

- six x 800m in 1:51 to 1:56 with about 90 seconds' recovery.

But this does not mean you should be drawn into such speed endurance efforts. It should be remembered that this is a key session for a top-level athlete preparing for a specific championship. It is hardly the sort of workout that he would be completing every week. The athlete that reads such sessions and tries to copy will break down quickly. It is important that you select the pace according to your ability at the time and make sure that the recovery is specific to the demands of the session and the time of year. Early-season work will be slower, and you should progress to quicker work, compensated by longer recovery to maintain the quality.

The physiological adaptations to this type of anaerobic endurance training take place within the muscle. The enzymes that control the chemical reactions to produce energy start to work in a more efficient manner. Lactate tolerance is also improved within the working muscles.

Planning your anaerobic training in advance is the only way to achieve your best. This may mean training alone sometimes, but if you want to get the best out of yourself, rather than simply be the best in your training group, you may have to plan and go it alone. So, before you head off for the track this season think first of what you want to train, and then think whether the session you are about to tackle is really going to challenge the body in the way to take you to your peak performance.

Joe Dunbar

Module 7

Psychology

Introduction

The increased stress of competitions can cause athletes to react both physically and mentally in a manner which can negatively affect their performance abilities. They may become tense, their heart rate races, they break into a cold sweat, they worry about the outcome of the competition, they find it hard to concentrate on the task in hand.

This has led coaches to take an increasing interest in the field of sports psychology and in particular in the area of competitive anxiety. That interest has focused on techniques which athletes can use in the competitive situation to maintain control and optimise their performance. Once learned, these techniques allow the athlete to relax and to focus their attention in a positive manner on the task of preparing for and participating in competition.

Overview of the psychology module

In this module we look at how psychology can help improve sporting performances.

- Lee Crust explains what to think about when you are training and competing.
- Daniel Bishop explains how the use of imagery can help your performance.
- Daniel Bishop outlines a 10-point plan to help make imagery work for you.
- Lee Crust identifies strategies to control your pre-competition emotions.
- Raphael Brandon explains how team cohesion and success go together.

All the articles in this module are applicable to most sports.

When it comes to doing your best, it is the thoughts that count

When it comes to running, or any other endurance sport, your mind can be your biggest asset or your worst enemy. Enjoying your training and achieving your best performance is not simply down to physical conditioning: your mental state and particularly the thoughts that run through your mind can affect the way you feel during exercise. It is normal for athletes to plan their race strategy in minute detail, but how many systematically plan what they are going to think about during training or competition?

Having worked with and questioned athletes on their thoughts over a number of years, I can tell you that the number who do plan their thoughts is surprisingly small. I say surprising because, as a sports psychologist, I am aware of what scientific research has been showing for a number of years: that thoughts do matter. In fact the nature and quality of your thoughts can make the difference between winning and losing, enjoying or hating your training, and may even impact on your decision to stay with an exercise programme.

Much of this scientific evidence comes from studies of marathon runners. Neuroscientists have shown that we have thousands of thoughts running through our minds each and every day. Athletes spend a large percentage of their time thinking sport-related thoughts, but most of these are unplanned and random. The first step towards becoming more organised and purposeful in your thinking is to become more aware of them. So when you next go for a training run, cycle or swim, try to become more aware of what you are thinking about.

Association and dissociation

So what should you be thinking about? Two very different mental strategies have emerged, both commonly used by elite and other runners. *Association* involves focusing on bodily sensations and monitoring any changes, usually internal, that occur. Breathing rate and muscular sensations provide physiological cues that allow you to pace yourself with a view to avoiding or minimising pain.

By contrast, *dissociation* is about directing attention away from bodily sensations by a form of distraction designed to reduce the athlete's awareness of fatigue or effort. This can be achieved by many means, including music. However, more 'active' strategies like counting tasks or the alphabet game (see table 1) might be more effective.

Table 1 - Techniques for dissociation

1. **Music** – This can generate positive thoughts, improve your mood state and distract you from the physical demands of your sport. But be careful not to get too distracted if you are running in a busy area.

2. **Counting game** – Count the number of blue cars you see, or the number of dogs or postboxes. Be inventive.

3. **Alphabet game** – Work through from A to Z for a chosen category, such as women's names or countries.

4. **Rainbow game** – Try to notice as many colours as possible while you work out: aim for all the colours of the rainbow.

5. **Active fantasy** – Imagine yourself as a lottery winner and decide how to spend your winnings.

Avoid thoughts relating to your work, jobs you have to do and anything problematic, as this can increase tension. Try to be creative and have fun with dissociation. It can help you relax and enjoy your sport even more.

I am often asked which of these strategies is best. There is no simple answer, but a recent review of scientific research in this area came to the following conclusions:

- in general, association appears to be linked to faster running times
- dissociation can reduce the sense of effort and awareness of physical sensations such as pain and fatigue, usually up to moderate to high intensity
- athletes of all levels appear to favour association in competition and dissociation in training
- elite athletes tend to use both strategies during training and races, and are able to switch between the two, as required.

When trying to decide which strategy might be best for you, it is important to consider your personal situation, preferences and goals. For example, most athletes perform training runs at a slower pace than they use in competition, making body monitoring less essential. A better goal for training might be to relieve boredom and monotony, in which case dissociation, with active mental processing, might be most beneficial. Dissociation may also benefit athletes who want to improve their endurance by running or exercising for longer at moderate intensities.

However, because dissociation works by distracting the mind, it might work against an athlete setting an ideal pace for optimum performance. The reason why association appears so important in competition is that by monitoring bodily responses an athlete can ride that thin line between pushing for maximum performance and overdoing it.

Association involves entering a more concentrated state when you can react to changes within your body. Focusing on internal states, like rhythmical breathing, can help you feel more relaxed during physical activity (see table 2). But on the downside, there is some evidence of a link between association and injury. Some athletes, it appears, choose to associate with pain and fatigue-related symptoms and end up pushing themselves too hard.

Table 2 - Techniques for associative body-monitoring: follow this three-stage plan

1. Focus on your breathing. Controlled, relatively deep rhythmic breathing is the key to relaxation. When you breathe out, try to imagine the tension leaving your body.
2. Try to remain relaxed while running (or cycling or swimming), but be aware of tension and fatigue in your muscles. It is often a good idea to start from the head and work down, giving each area or group of muscles your attention. If you notice tension, try to focus on a cue-word, such as 'relax' or 'easy' to let the tension flow out of the muscles.
3. Keep your pace in line with the information you gain from body-monitoring. You might, for example, increase the pace if you feel very positive. Repeat the monitoring constantly or, alternatively, take some time out for dissociation. You might also reinforce your mood by telling yourself how well you are doing and that you need to keep working hard and remain focused.

Most successful elite marathon runners have been shown to combine associative and dissociative strategies when planning their thoughts. There are times, especially in races, when you need to be very aware of your own physical state and of events in the external environment. However, there are also times when you can plan to 'switch off' and give yourself a break from the mental demands of competition or training. The best thing is to construct a plan with your coach, exercise leader or even a more experienced fellow athlete. Try to decide between you what the best approach is for you, and plan what you will be thinking about during the race or training sessions.

For a 30-minute training run, you might decide on cyclic phases of thinking, *eg* 10 minutes of body monitoring, 10 minutes of alphabet game, then more body monitoring to the end. It is all perfectly logical once you get started. You would not leave your physical preparations to chance, so why allow your thoughts to crop up in random fashion?

Learn to script your internal dialogue

When running, cycling or swimming for long periods of time, the mind can wander freely, if you let it. When this happens, your natural internal dialogue, or self-talk, becomes important. If your concentration does stray, or your body monitoring detects fatigue, it is vital that your self-talk remains positive. The best thing is to avoid over-emotional self-talk and focus on self-instructing, motivational content. To this end, you can plan and even rehearse what you are going to say to yourself beforehand, just as you might rehearse an important telephone call or speech. The key is to stay positive even when the situation is less than ideal. This is not an easy feat to pull off and will take some time to master.

The first step in this process is to become more aware of your thoughts during training and competition. If you want to gain more control over your thoughts, try to formulate a simple plan and try it out over a number of weeks during training. If you notice any undesirable patterns in your thinking, such as negative self-talk or loss of focus, you can try to combat these by planning more positive alternative thoughts. You can, for example, frame positive statements that you repeat to yourself regularly. Ideally, write these statements down and place them in prominent positions where you cannot avoid seeing them. Work on recalling these statements when you become aware of negative thoughts or feelings. This might seem a little strange at first, but you are actually programming your brain to notice more 'positives' and, over time, this will become a habit.

Athletes often recall that their very best performances are accompanied by few thoughts, a feeling of complete control, effortless movements and a sense of being 'on automatic pilot'. Sport psychologists often refer to this as a 'state of flow'. The aspects of positive thinking and focus discussed in this article have been shown to increase the likelihood of achieving flow, although environmental factors can also be important.

Do not leave your psychological preparation to chance. Remember that you control your thoughts, not the other way round. The way you think is strongly linked to the way you perform. So if you want to perform better, gain greater control and enjoy your sport more, start planning today because, in this sphere, the thoughts really do count.

Lee Crust

How to think your way into a winning performance

A 1988 survey undertaken by Orlick and Partington revealed that 99% of the 235 elite athletes in their sample used mental imagery for performance preparation. A report the following year by Jowdy, Murphy and Durtschi at a US Olympic Training Center showed that 90% of their respondents used imagery for training and competition and 94% of coaches reported using imagery with their athletes. Professional British athletes from Sally Gunnell to Rob Andrew have used imagery to prepare just before competitions. The positive effects of imagery are well documented in the scientific literature, and it continues to be one of the hot topics in sports psychology.

Imagery is commonly referred to as 'mental practice' or 'mental rehearsal' because it normally involves 'going through the motions' of your sport in your head. There are a number of aspects of the process that are widely considered necessary for imagery to be effective. Here I will briefly introduce the relevant theory behind imagery and its purported effects, together with some empirical evidence for its potential benefits.

Psycho-neuromuscular theory

This theory maintains that during imagery the motor programme for a given activity is run, albeit at a lower level, in the correct sequential order. In other words, the neurons fire in the same pattern as during the physical action but at a level not great enough to produce movement. The physical implications of this theory mean that it is easy to test.

Some of the earliest work on psycho-neuromuscular theory was done by Jacobsen (1930) using electromyography, a technique for measuring intramuscular electrical activity. He found that the electromyographic (EMG) activity during imagery of a physical action mirrored the EMG of the actual execution of the action itself, although at a greatly reduced amplitude. Similar findings have been produced in more recent studies. For instance, Bakker, Boschker and Chung (1996) asked subjects in their study to image the performance of a biceps curl with both a 9kg dumbbell and a 4.5kg dumbbell. EMG activity was significantly greater in the 'active' arm when lifting a 9kg dumbbell was imaged, and the comparison EMG measure in the 'passive' arm was significantly less, regardless of weight, implying that the muscular activity during imagery was also specific to the muscle that would normally be active in executing the task.

Try this experiment

The mind-body link in action can be demonstrated fairly easily by the 'string and bolt' method. Suspend a bolt, or any object of comparable weight, from a piece of string about 20cm in length. Tie the free end of the string around one forefinger and place the elbow of the same arm on a solid surface, bent at an angle of about 45 degrees, suspending the newly created pendulum in mid-air. While making sure that you keep your arm absolutely still, try to feel the movements that the muscles of your forearm would need to make in order to swing the pendulum back and forth. It is essential to concentrate hard. Now feel yourself bringing the pendulum to a halt, then moving it from side to side, then in a clockwise circle, then anti-clockwise – the order is immaterial.

Virtually everyone who tries this experiment will see the pendulum move in the direction imaged, and see it stop on command, without a conscious attempt to move it. There is no 'trick' to this, it is a very real psycho-neuromuscular phenomenon. The signals from your brain are strong enough to elicit the correct muscle movements, imperceptible to the naked eye, such that the pendulum itself moves.

Now ask yourself precisely which muscles you would consciously use, and in what order, to bring about the pendulum swings. It becomes clear (unless you are an expert in the kinesiology of the lower arm) that imagery allows us access to the motor programmes for a variety of actions, the instructions for which are not consciously accessible. These can be the sorts of skill that you as an athlete perform automatically to varying degrees, *eg* the tennis player making a reaction stop volley or the distance runner whose every movement is taking place on auto-pilot. Thus imagery is capable of fine-tuning movements that we may take for granted as being 'as good as they can be'. Improved motor-neuron recruitment could mean the difference between hitting a winner or the net, or between first and second place.

Feel it... do it

Along with the procedure for the string and bolt method, there exists an important distinction between two types of imagery perspective, internal and external. The internal perspective is 'first-person imagery', in which you imagine the activity as if you were physically going through the motions. The internal perspective provides us with a great deal of sensory information not afforded by the external perspective, aka 'third-person imagery'. This means a visual approach to imagery, as if you were an external observer, or watching yourself on videotape. The instructions I gave for the string and bolt demonstration were from an internal perspective. Referring back to the instructions, remove the focus from the muscles of the forearm and substitute the word 'see' for 'feel'. All of a sudden the perspective has switched to an external viewpoint. Many experts believe the internal perspective to be the most effective. The content of an imagery programme is thus crucial to its effectiveness, and Lang's (1989) Bio Informational theory accordingly addresses this aspect.

Bio Informational theory

This theory maintains that the brain is cognitively organised into discrete compartments containing finite sets of propositions, each containing information about the characteristics and interrelationships of various stimuli and their associated physical/behavioural responses. Stimulus propositions hold information about the external environment, such as the ambient temperature, the presence of opponents, the sound of a starter's pistol, etc, or salient contextual information, such as the importance of the competition. Response propositions describe one's response to these external stimuli, such as changes in heart rate, limb movements, feelings of anxiety and apprehension. In order for a response proposition to be elicited, a sufficient number and quality of stimulus propositions must be activated.

According to Lang, when a cognitive mapping is made between a stimulus response pair, the connection between them can be either reinforced or modified according to the desirability of the outcome. More often than not, during imagery training, a sports psychologist would be responsible for describing and/or developing what is known as the imagery 'script', whether it is tape-recorded or spoken. The skill of the psychologist in constructing this script thus determines its effectiveness. In the string and bolt example, the word 'feel' constitutes use of a response proposition, in contrast to 'see', which is a stimulus proposition. Many researchers agree that there is an inextricable link between external/internal perspectives and the use of stimulus/response propositions, respectively.

In the study mentioned earlier by Frank Bakker and his colleagues, I neglected one important detail. The researchers manipulated the instructions so that half of the subjects were asked to 'see' themselves performing the task, while the other half were asked to 'feel' the movements. The subjects in the first group actually displayed no greater EMG when asked to picture the lift than they did at baseline. In other words, if increased motor neuron activity is our goal, then response propositions seem to be more effective.

Symbolic learning theory

This theory (Sackett, 1935) suggests that a 'mental blueprint' is formulated for any given activity and that the neurological connections for this blueprint can be strengthened by imagery. In essence the blueprint is a mental map of the movements required to execute a new skill. These mental maps are initially created by physical training and are bolstered by a combination of mental and physical practice.

Symbolic learning theory mostly holds true for cognitive rather than motor tasks. It is primarily focused on the skill-learning function of imagery. For example, the theory maintains that a move in judo or gymnastics would benefit more from imagery training than a less cognitive task such as running. However, activities like running may gain considerable benefit from the 'psyching-up' function of imagery, which brings me to my last theory.

Activation/arousal theory

This specifies that imagery establishes an optimal level of psychological arousal by arriving at a 'preparatory set' to enhance either learning or performance, depending on the type of activity to be undertaken. Thus, imagery for physical preparation should occur immediately before the execution of the skill in question. Evidence indicates that certain performance preparation tactics can be more suitable for some skills than others. For example, performance preparation for an endurance event, such as a marathon canoe or running race, would differ extensively from that applied to a briefer and more directed activity such as a jumping or throwing event. The idea of developing an optimal level of arousal is by no means new, and goes back at least as far as the often cited inverted-U hypothesis of Yerkes and Dodson in 1908.

It has also been suggested that varying levels of arousal are required for different sports. Gross motor activities such as running, cycling and swimming require psyching-up/high arousal, while fine motor tasks such as golf putting require lower arousal, perhaps through relaxation imagery. Thus, while Michael Johnson conjures up images of power and explosiveness at the start line, Tiger Woods may be using his walk up to the 18th green at Augusta to picture his 'quiet place', in order to steady his trembling arms and reduce the sweat pouring from his palms.

Take some REST

There is compelling evidence that 'reduced environmental stimulation therapy' (REST), usually in the form of flotation, increases the effectiveness of imagery. Research suggests that the sensory deprivation brought about by REST can facilitate a host of positive physical, physiological and behavioural changes, all of which help to improve the value of imaging.

One study of 22 elite college basketball players (by Wagaman, Barabasz and Barabasz in 1991) compared free throw shooting imagery during flotation REST to an imagery-only control group. The float group showed significantly higher scores than the controls on an objective performance measure (number of free throws scored). This suggests that REST can help make imagery more successful. If you do not have access to a flotation tank, a darkened room may do (take the phone off the hook!).

Get in tune with your body

I must admit to noticing something of a contradiction: how do athletes achieve this 'switching off', when all around them is buzzing? I have conducted recent research into the efficacy of pairing music with imagery training in recreational runners, with extremely promising results.

Participants in the study were randomly allocated to an imagery-training condition, imagery-plus-music condition, or a no-imagery control group.

Participants were tested for imagery ability at maximal treadmill running performance at both pre- and post-intervention. The same music as used in the imagery-plus-music condition was played during the warm-up before treadmill running at both times of testing.

The runners in the music group performed significantly better at maximal treadmill running than did the imagery-only or control group. Not only this, but kinaesthetic/internal imagery ability improved in both intervention groups as opposed to their non-imaging counterparts.

My explanation for the effects of music on performance is strikingly simple. Classical conditioning is probably the most famous of all learning theories. An unconditioned stimulus (UCS, the imagery training) may bring about an unconditioned response (UCR). The UCR in this study was hypothesised to manifest itself as physiological changes in the athlete such as increased peripheral blood flow to muscle structures or increased motor-neuron activation.

During the process of classical conditioning, a neutral stimulus, the conditioned stimulus (CS), is continually paired with the UCR, such that the learner begins to make an association between the CS and the UCR. After a matter of time, the CS presented alone is enough to elicit the response, this time known as the conditioned response (CR).

In this study, the music acts as the CS, also serving as the 'condensing' of all the information obtained from a relatively long imagery session into a much smaller segment. In addition, because of the ease with which musical tunes are recalled and recognised, it provides a strong and durable CS. Thus, it may well be advisable to continually pair a favourite tune with 'psyching-up' of activation imagery training and then to play the same tune immediately before a physical performance.

However, the effectiveness of this practice is wholly dependent on the skill with which the imagery script is constructed, and this is an art in its own right.

Daniel Bishop

A training script for an endurance runner, plus a 10-point plan for making imagery work

The following article is aimed at increasing physiological arousal in an endurance runner. It would take place following a thorough introduction to the requisite muscle groups and their functions. Some of the salient aspects of an imagery script are put in brackets for easy identification to enable you to refer back.

(REST) 'Before starting, I would like to remind you that you are seated in a comfortable chair in a quiet room with no distractions, including bright lights. Your arms and legs should be rested comfortably, with your head supported. If there are other things on your mind, or something is bothering you, you must first resolve these problems before continuing with this script.'

(Breathing exercise, optional) 'To begin with, develop a relaxed breathing style. You may find it helpful to close your eyes through the entire programme, including this breathing exercise. Breathing in slowly through your nose, first allow your stomach and then your chest to expand outwards, drawing as much air as possible into the lungs. Allow the shoulders to lift gently as your breathing deepens. When you can draw in no more, allow the air to pass slowly from your mouth as your chest and stomach recede and your shoulders sink.'

'Close your eyes if they are not already closed; imagine being by yourself on a cross-country training run, running briskly through woodland and miles from any cars or buildings.'

(Multi-sensory information) 'It is a warm spring morning and the sun is shining hazily through the canopy of trees and drifting clouds. Feel its gentle warmth on the nape of your neck (Proprioceptive). You can also feel the slightest of breezes flickering across your forehead, keeping you perfectly cool (Proprioceptive). You are miles from anyone, with only the birds for company. Feel and hear (Auditory) the soft soil and woodchips crunching lightly under your feet with each stride. The scenery whizzes by, everything becomes blurred into a palette of serene colour (Visual). The colours of spring leap out at you, greens, browns, reds. Small flowers add dashes of intense colour to the peaceful backdrop of the woodland. Smell their scent (Olfactory). It urges you to take in deeper breaths. As a result, your breathing is deep and slow. The air today is richer than usual, rich with energy-giving oxygen. Picture the bright red, oxygen-rich blood surging around your body. Huge volumes course through your large thigh and buttock muscles. This is reflected in the feeling of warmth in them – they are supple and strong, and exude power. This is a run you wish could go on forever, knowing that you can never feel tired in this euphoric state.'

(External perspective) 'Look at yourself now as an outsider would see you. The stride pattern of your legs: quick drives forward and then strong pulls against the ground, propelling you forwards. Notice the uprightness of your posture and the protrusion of your chest as your powerful arms drive back and forth like highly

efficient pistons. Think of how effortlessly and efficiently your arms and legs work together and the power that your muscles generate. You feel energised; you feel strong and relaxed and transcend everything around you. Your arms and legs burst you forward. For all intents and purposes, your body is a highly specialised machine, each of its parts working together in absolute synchrony. Electricity is flowing around your body, surging from a seemingly endless supply.'

(Internal perspective) 'Think of one of your arms only, how it feels as it describes its arc through the air. The posterior head of your deltoid and your latissimus dorsi contract to swing the arm sharply backward. Just at that moment, electrical signals from your brain tell the fibres of your pectorals and those in your anterior deltoid to contract in order to propel your arm forward with force. At the end of the drive forward, these muscle fibres are maximally contracted and begin to relax as the signals tell the latissimus dorsi and posterior fibres of your deltoid to take over again. All this time, the musculature of the opposite arm is working in perfect synchrony, so that one arm is always providing you with force in a forward direction. Your arms seem to move through their own channels. These channels have no air resistance whatsoever, and your arms fly through them with consummate ease. Your upper body is still, it makes no movements; it is a strong base for your arms to work from. It is as though you are caught in a trance. Everything around you is superfluous, irrelevant.'

'You are running alongside a stream, which ripples incessantly. The fast-moving water compels you to compete. Feel your strides quicken as your powerful hip flexors contract, feel the strong muscles in your shoulders driving you onwards. All of a sudden, the stream changes its course to veer sharply across your path (*stimulus proposition*), forcing you to jump over the water. Your body lowers slightly and your stride lengthens in order to gain additional lift and thrust; you swing your arms in exaggerated arcs. At takeoff, your quads and glutes contract powerfully (*response propositions*) in perfect unison, propelling you upwards and forwards, sending you clear of the stream. Your arms swing sharply forward to give added momentum, jack-knifing you at the waist. Your body coils to absorb the impact on the other side, before easing back into your stride.'

Clearly, a good knowledge of your sport is important in order to construct a good imagery script. The more relevant sensory images you can evoke, the more effective the script will be. The content will also differ depending on the aim of the programme, *eg* arousal versus skill learning, and the type of sport. For instance, an imagery script for hockey requires considerable perspective switching and greater emphasis on cognitive processes than, say, a script for running. However, regardless of your sport, the following 10-point plan should help make your imagery more effective.

The top 10 plan for ideal imagery

1. Develop an imagery script on cassette to use as a focal point if your motivation and/or training are waning. If you are unhappy with your own voice, ask a dulcet-toned friend to do the recording. To give an idea of script length and the time taken, speaking at 165 words per minute enables easy comprehension and assimilation of information. Thus a 12-minute recording will require a script slightly longer than this article. Perhaps even more effective would be audio imagery combined with video modelling by someone else. This is known as 'vicarious experience' (sympathetic understanding of another's experience) and is a major precursor of self-efficacy (situation-specific self-confidence) for performing a given task. It is important that the person in the video is of a comparable skill and appearance and that the execution of the skills is correct. In this way, video modelling can provide not only learning but also motivational benefits – *ie*, if they can do it, so can I.

2. For most sports, use an internal imagery perspective. Concentrate on the feelings associated with your sport. If it has a technical orientation, especially if you are graded according to presentation, as in gymnastics, use the external way of imaging. Remember, however, that imagery perspective is partly a natural attribute and people vary in their favoured perspective. In fact, most athletes switch perspectives naturally throughout imagery.

3. Make the internal imagery multi-sensory, *ie* incorporating all the senses: visual, auditory, olfactory (smell), proprioceptive (touch, balance and movement) and gustatory (taste). The thicker the description you can summon up in your imagery script, the more effective it will be. Use plenty of superlatives and descriptions of positive mood.

4. Image in real time. Some research has shown that slow-motion imagery elicits very different muscle EMG from real-time imaging and thus may not be as beneficial.

5. Remember to include significant stimulus response pairings. Examples are the sound of the crowd cheering, your coach giving last-minute instructions, the smell of dew before a very important race coupled with the resultant butterflies in the stomach, a slight rush of adrenaline, the feeling of pressure and anxiety, a dry mouth, and so on. Again, your choice of pairings needs careful thought.

6. Incorporate REST (reduced environmental stimulation therapy, such as flotation) into your imagery training. The mind should be undisturbed and uncluttered.

7. Imagery ability is a major factor in making it work. Ability comes with practice and time spent on mental training can be just as important as that devoted to physical work. Ten minutes three times a week can bring a wealth of benefits.

8. If you want a method of translating all of your imagery practice into a pre-competition routine, try pairing a favourite tune with each imagery session, so that playing the tune may evoke all the associated

physiological and behavioural changes. For best results, choose music that you personally find motivating, making you feel energised.

9. From a learning point of view, imagery coupled with actual execution of the task has been shown to be more effective for skill acquisition than imagery on its own. Thus it would make sense to undertake imagery training immediately before physical training, though this may cause some REST problems.

10. One final tip is to use biofeedback – most conveniently, in the form of a personal heart rate monitor to assess your progress. Research has shown that biofeedback can heighten and quicken learning during imagery training. Learn to associate relaxing imagery with lowered heart rate, and arousal imagery, *eg* pre-competition psyching up, with increased heart rate.

Finally and most importantly, do not expect miraculous improvements overnight. Be patient with mental training and apply the above tenets regularly. Successful imagery can be rewarding in many aspects of life as well as sport and exercise.

Daniel Bishop

References

Bakker, FC, Boschker, MSJ, and Chung, T (1996), 'Changes in muscular activity while imagining weight lifting using stimulus or response propositions', *The Journal of Sport & Exercise Psychology,* 18, pp313-324

Bull, SJ, Albinson, JG, and Shambrook, J (1996), *The Mental Game Plan: Getting Psyched for Sport.* Brighton: Sports Dynamics

Jowdy, Murphy and Durtschi (1989), 'Report on the United States Olympic Committee survey on imagery use in sport.' Colorado Springs, CO: US Olympic Training Center

Munroe, Hall, Sims and Weinberg (1998), 'The influence of type of sport and time of season on athletes' use of imagery', *The Sport Psychologist,* 12, pp440-449

Murphy, SM and Jowdy, DP (1992), 'Imagery and mental practice'. In: Horn, IS (Ed) *Advances in Sport Psychology*, pp221-250. Champaign, IL: Human Kinetics Orlick, T, and Partington, J (1988), 'Mental links to excellence', *The Sport Psychologist,* 2, pp105-130

Syer, J, and Connolly, C (1998), *Sporting body, sporting mind: An athlete's guide to mental training.* London: Simon and Schuster

Vadocz, EA, Hall, CR, and Moritz, SE (1997), 'The relationship between competitive anxiety and imagery use', *Journal of Applied Sport Psychology,* 9, pp241-252

Use these pre-performance strategies to take control of your emotions (before they take control of you)

Competition can bring out the best or the worst in athletes, and the psychological demands are especially high when individuals or teams are striving to achieve the same goals. When physical skills are evenly matched, it is often the competitor with the stronger mental approach, the one who can control his or her mind before and during events, who wins. However, many athletes wrongly assume that mental aspects of performance are innate and unchangeable when in reality, systematic mental training can have a similar impact on performance as physical workouts.

Getting into the correct mind-set prior to competition is one of the most crucial aspects of top performance. In fact, a study of Olympic athletes by Orlick and Partington[1] showed that the combination of mental and physical readiness was a key factor that distinguished more successful athletes from their less successful counterparts in the Olympic Games. Perhaps even more impressive is the finding that, of the three states of readiness assessed (mental, physical and technical) only mental factors were statistically linked with final Olympic rankings.

If you have ever observed performers during the lead-up to competition, you cannot have failed to notice that behaviour starts to change. As the anticipation builds, athletes and coaches cope with the demands of the situation in various ways, some becoming withdrawn and quiet and some more aggressive than usual, while others disappear frequently to the toilet. Emotional reactions to stressful situations can drain an athlete's resources and impact negatively on performance if poorly managed. That is why it is important to have in place a strategy to deal with pre-performance stress.

Triggers for emotions

Emotions can be defined as brief positive or negative feelings occurring in response to meaningful or important situations, which can influence mood states. Basic emotions such as fear, anger, joy and surprise are commonly experienced in sport, although complex mixes of emotions are often evident. Positive emotions can help sustain motivation and enable us to approach events with enthusiasm and energy. Negative emotions, by contrast, are linked to avoidance behaviours and withdrawal. Emotions in the sporting arena can be triggered by many things personal to an individual, including memories, conversations with other people, seeing the competition venue, weighing up the opposition, etc.

Researchers have studied emotions in order to determine why they occur and what impact they have on behaviour. At first it was thought that emotions were simply the result of physiological changes, since physiological symptoms such as increased heart rate were commonly observed in such reactions. To test this theory, scientists injected volunteers with the so-called 'stress' hormone epinephrine (adrenaline) to see if emotions could be generated in the laboratory.

A small minority of participants reported feeling genuine emotions (usually sadness) while most reported physiological changes (to be expected after administration of adrenaline) and 'as if' emotions – feelings closely associated with being happy, sad or angry, but not the 'real thing[2].'

Best friend or worst enemy?

Subsequent research demonstrated that emotions could be induced by directing participants' thoughts to emotional triggers, such as deceased relatives (sadness) or past achievements (pride). In summary, research in these areas has shown that both physiological arousal and the cognitive interpretation of that arousal are important in determining the emotional response.

During the lead-up to an important competition, the body starts to prepare for the demands to come by releasing hormones such as epinephrine into the bloodstream, setting in motion the physiological changes associated with increased arousal (sometimes referred to as the 'fight or flight' response). In addition, changes occur in the attentional system, as athletes become more focused and alert, with increasingly active minds. This overall increase in arousal can be your best friend or your worst enemy. The key to achieving an appropriate mind-set is to analyse the changes in a rational manner and channel your emotions in a positive direction.

Many elite athletes associate increased arousal with excitement as the body readies itself for competition and use it as a cue to focus on pre-planned routines. This positive interpretation of the arousal response usually leads to more positive emotions and optimistic outlooks. Conversely, some athletes interpret physiological changes like an increased heart rate as anxiety, worry and apprehension, with a negative impact on emotions that is not conducive to good performance.

The most important thing to remember is that your interpretation of physiological changes directs your emotional response. However, the relationship between thoughts and emotions works in both directions. Although emotions are the result of cognitive interpretations, they can also impact on your thoughts, giving rise to a vicious circle of negative thoughts and emotions.

The good news for athletes who experience unhelpful emotions before competition is that you can gain more control by altering your focus of attention. The next time you feel these unwanted changes occurring, try going through the following psychological routine:

1. Tell yourself 'this is my body preparing me to perform well' and repeat the affirmation as necessary.
2. Try to recall an image of yourself either winning or performing well and connect this with the feelings you experienced at the time.

You will need to practise this routine on a regular basis in order to establish it as a habitual response that will help you feel more composed and energised before competitions. If negative images jump into your mind during this time, try to visualise the most successful athlete in your sport and the way he or she runs, competes and enjoys performing. In short every positive thing about them. Then visualise yourself with similar positive attributes.

Even experienced athletes get nervous and irritable before competing and a little tension (as long as it is controlled) is often necessary to inspire maximal performance. The techniques outlined above will not remove all the tension, but they should help you to channel your emotions more positively, which is what top athletes have to learn to do. The difference between winners and losers often boils down to coping skills, in that some athletes have learned to cope with competitive situations better than others.

It is important to challenge the belief of some athletes that emotions and mood states are simply reactions to external events. In fact, the athlete has considerable capacity for control in this area. A recent study by Stevens and Lane identified a number of strategies employed by athletes to regulate their moods[3]. Although unique strategies were employed for specific mood dimensions, results indicated that 'changing location' and 'listening to music' were among the most commonly used strategies. Various research studies have demonstrated the ability of music to impact on emotions and mood by either calming or stimulating the individual as required, although careful consideration is needed in the selection of appropriate music. Listening to music or engaging in a mentally active process, such as a crossword, can help to stop the mind wandering in the hours leading up to competition, although immediately beforehand athletes need to be completely focused on the task in hand.

Having worked with sportsmen and women who have experienced emotional disturbance prior to competing, I believe that mental preparation needs are highly varied. The common approach that I have found successful is to develop with each athlete a coping response that becomes automated and can be consistently applied in changing circumstances. Such a coping response puts the athlete in control by creating a familiar psychological comfort zone regardless of whatever is going on in the external environment.

One of the biggest triggers for anxiety is uncertainty – which is, of course, inherent in all sporting events. The key principle for the athlete is to control the things you can control but not to waste energy on things you cannot. Many top athletes have found, to their cost, that giving attention to how opponents might perform or how technically good others were in the warm-up has a negative impact on their focus. The one thing you can control is your own preparation, so that should have your full focus. By developing consistent routines and ways of coping with distractions, uncertainty can be reduced and you are less likely to be negatively affected by external factors.

Because athletes have varying requirements, it is impossible to standardise the pre-competition preparation. However, you may wish to adopt some of the ideas below in creating your own pre-performance strategy to achieve the desired emotional state. These ideas are all designed to be put into practice in the hour before competition, although the principles can be adapted for other times.

Physical preparation

The warm-up period can be an important psychological aid as well as preparing the body for the rigours of competition and helping to prevent injury. Remember the comfort zone? By developing a relatively stable warm-up routine, including mobility work, stretching and increasing deep muscle temperature, uncertainty can be reduced and the athlete's attention directed to appropriate cues, such as quality technique and body awareness. The development of routines in sport has consistently been shown to be important in directing attentional focus to important cues, so aiding performance.

Although during the last major athletic event it was impossible to observe what was going on inside the minds of the sprinters, you could clearly observe the regularity of the warm-up routines and the intense concentration written on athletes' faces prior to taking their marks. These routines are not haphazard, but have been systematically designed to promote optimal functioning in the final few minutes before performance.

Golfers have routines that allow them to prepare in the same way for each shot, as do some rugby place kickers and tennis players before serving. The key to any routine is that it provides the athlete with control and directs attention to the important cues. Coaches and athletes should work together in deciding the key attentional cues and the sequence in which these should occur. Such routines are the opposite of superstitious rituals that take control away from the performer; with superstitions, the outcome is essentially believed to be controlled by sources other than the self.

Mental preparation

The mental aspects prior to performance should involve focusing on what you are going to do during the event. This can include specific strategies and the establishment of optimal attentional focus. Some athletes will use imagery to recall positive past experiences and generate a sense of confidence. Imagery is a very flexible method to employ prior to competition, but it needs to be used correctly for maximum effect. Imagery is not just a form of visualisation, but an all-sensory experience that should involve the kinaesthetic senses, emotions and auditory experiences to increase the impact. Many people use imagery simply to see themselves winning but it can be employed to imagine good technique, coping with difficult situations, recreating emotional feelings and rehearsing the upcoming event in the mind. Imagery is a powerful technique since the brain interprets the imagined scenarios very literally, directly enhancing such psychological variables as confidence.

Always keep imagery sessions short (no more than a few minutes) and simple just before competition. Tailoring the imagery to the desired outcome is essential, so if you want to improve your mood, imagine a realistic scenario that makes you feel good. For more advice on incorporating imagery into your preparation, you may like to read a very practical book entitled *In Pursuit of Excellence*[4].

Mental preparation can include the repeated use of positive self-statements (affirmations) such as 'I have trained hard and am in great shape'. These affirmations act by occupying our attention in such a way as to change our belief system over time, so that we begin to attend to feelings or happenings that are consistent with these new beliefs. In the example given above, we begin to focus on events that reinforce our belief that we are in great shape, such as a fast training run. In this way negative perceptions can be tuned out.

The 'quick set' routine

Psychologist Jeff Simons has described one of the best ways to organise the last 20 to 30 seconds before competition in what has become known as the quick set routine[5]. This three-phase routine is designed to provide a quick focus that can be used just before competition or as a means of refocusing quickly following a distraction. It is minimal in content, which appeals to many athletes, and involves a physical, emotional and focus cue. An example for a sprinter could be:

1. Close your eyes, clear your mind and maintain deep rhythmical breathing, in through your nose and out through your mouth (physical cue).
2. Imagine a previous race win, see yourself crossing the line first and recreate those feelings (emotional cue).
3. Return your focus to the sprint start, thinking of blasting off on the 'B' of the bang (focus cue).

However meticulous your planning, things often occur at the competition site that are out of your control. Such events have the potential to impact on your emotional state, distract you from your goals and push you out of your optimal state of preparedness. However, it is important to remember that things only become distractions if you let them. They do not have to negatively influence your mood if you can learn to let them go and refocus.

Why Sugar Ray Leonard lost it in more ways than one

Distractions can by provided by your opponents. It is increasingly common for opponents to use psych-out strategies or mind games to try and break your concentration and consistency. Comments such as: 'I'm surprised to see you competing so soon after that injury' are attempts to divert your attention away from your preparation and towards negative memories and self-doubt.

The best strategy with such comments is to ignore them, although that is easier said than done. If you feel yourself paying attention to them, it is important to become aware that you have lost your optimal focus and need to refocus quickly. First, 'let go' of the distraction and put it out of your mind; say to yourself 'let it go', shake down your body, and refocus on your breathing. Some people might prefer to use their quick set routine to refocus in such circumstances.

Remember that some opponents are actively seeking to unsettle you and that by reacting to their comments or behaviour you are falling into their trap and allowing them the psychological edge. By engaging in this psychological duel you run the risk of disrupting your emotional state, becoming over-aroused and suffering a catastrophic decline in performance that is difficult to recover from quickly. Reacting emotionally often means that you discard your carefully laid plans and operate a strategy of reprisal. Self-control is best regained by not reacting to provocation. This, in turn, can make your opponent worried or angry as it demonstrates that their attempts to undermine you have failed. Attempts to engage in such antics can, in any case, be a sign that your opponent is worried about you.

A classic example of how emotions can affect sport performers came in a famous 1980 boxing match between Sugar Ray Leonard and Roberto Duran. Leonard was considered the better boxer who was expected to outclass Duran with slick movements and long-range punching. However, before the fight Duran insulted Leonard in front of his family and this, to the dismay of Leonard's trainer Angelo Dundee, sent Leonard into a rage, which completely altered the course of subsequent events. Instead of fighting to the pre-planned strategy devised with his trainer, Leonard let his emotions take over and decided he was going to 'beat up' his opponent. Duran's actions amounted to a psychological masterstroke as Leonard ditched his boxing skills and opted for a brawl. It was exactly what Duran had hoped for and he won a points decision.

There are many other potential distractions for the athlete, including the actions of friends or family, coaches or team-mates, the environmental conditions, memories, delays and irrelevant thoughts. All of these can detract from your preparations, so be ready to clear your mind and refocus as necessary. Alternatively, remove yourself physically from the source of these distractions if possible.

Take time to learn

Learning any physical skill takes time, effort and practice. Psychological skills are no different in this respect, so do not expect miraculous overnight changes in your performance. If you are a serious athlete, it is best to work with your coach to devise routines and mental plans. Once you are happy with these, they can be introduced first to practice situations and later to competition.

Give yourself a few weeks to use these new techniques before re-evaluating them and adding or deleting parts as necessary. It is unlikely that the initial plans or routines will be perfect, so do not be afraid to develop them. It is also sensible to add distractions to your training sessions in order to simulate more realistic conditions. This can include attempting to refocus while people are trying to distract you. You might even practise your refocusing skills using imagery, by envisaging potential distracting scenarios in your mind. Only when you are comfortable with your strategies should you start to use them in competitions. Remember to give it time, as improvements take time to show through.

Emotions are an essential part of sport and competition, but if you do not gain control of them before competing they might control you and hinder your performance. While it is true that some people are more emotionally sensitive than others, taking mental charge by implementing psychological plans and routines can help all athletes to a more optimal state of readiness for performance.

Lee Crust

References

1. Orlick and Partington (1998), *The Sport Psychologist,* vol 2, pp105-130
2. *Personality and Social Psychology Bulletin*, vol 17, pp65-69
3. Stevens and Lane (2001), *Athletic-insight: the online journal of sport psychology,* vol 3 (3)
4. Terry Orlick (2000), *In Pursuit of Excellence,* Human Kinetics
5. *Track and Field Quarterly*, vol 92 (1), (1992)

Is there a link between team cohesion and success?

You may consider the above to be a question with a boringly obvious answer. Surely there must be a link between team cohesion and competition success? Anyone who has played in a team where everyone gets on well and communication is good feels this has a lot to do with how well the team plays.

However, this assumption is based on feelings and perceptions which may not be borne out in reality. Just because you enjoy the team atmosphere does not necessarily mean you are definitely going to win more games. The key research question for sports psychology is to prove that teams with greater cohesion are more successful. This is a question that various researchers have been grappling with for around 30 years.

Famously, a German researcher called Hans Lenk[1] disproved the notion that only cohesive groups could win by showing data collected from the notoriously dysfunctional German rowing eight that was successful in the 1968 Mexico

Olympic Games. Anecdotally, Olympic rowing provides another famous example of how low cohesion and success can mix, as 1988 GB gold medallists Holmes and Redgrave were supposedly not the best of pals. In subsequent Games (1992 and 1996), however, winners Redgrave and Pinsent were highly cohesive (from an outsider's viewpoint at least).

These examples cast doubt on the assumption that the greater the cohesion the greater the team success, although a reasonable amount of research carried out in the 1970s and 1980s supported this assumption[2]. But if the relationship between cohesion and success is not cut and dried, this raises more questions:

- If winning is possible without cohesion, how important is cohesion to the winning formula?
- Are there specific aspects of cohesion that are crucial for team success and others that are less important?

To provide reliable answers to these questions, psychology researchers need to be able to analyse and measure team cohesion with validity. In science, the term validity refers to how well your measuring tool actually assesses what you are aiming to measure. In physical terms a ruler is obviously a highly valid measure of length, but in the realms of psychology, in which variations in individual perceptions are involved, validity is not so easy to establish. A research team led by Albert Carron[3] concluded that much of the early research on cohesion was limited by the less than rigorous Sport Cohesiveness Questionnaire in use at the time. He and his colleagues set about developing a sounder tool, known as the Group Environment Questionnaire (GEQ).

These researchers aimed to base this new tool on a sound concept of what cohesion actually involved for sports teams. They argued that previous research had over-simplified the concept of cohesion by measuring one particular aspect, such as the perceived attraction of the group members to each other. There is clearly more to the dynamics of the formation and workings of groups than how much the individual members like each other.

Carron et al's model of cohesion identified four key contributing factors that interact to facilitate social or task cohesion: environmental, personal, team and leadership.

The model measures the following categories of cohesion:
1. individuals' perception of the 'group integration' (social)
2. individuals' personal attraction to 'group' (social)
3. individuals' perception of group task ('group integration task')
4. individuals' personal attraction to group task.

The GEQ comprises four or five questions under each category. Other research teams have endorsed Carron et al's belief that cohesion can be effectively measured by analysing its different components.

Interestingly, research into cohesion using the GEQ suggests that 'task' cohesion is more important for team success than 'social' cohesion. And this could explain the equivocal results of earlier cohesion studies and why it is sometimes possible for successful team-mates to actively dislike each other and still win. Most coaches and athletes prefer team-mates to like each other, but it appears that as long as they are completely focused on their common task and share the same goals and beliefs, success is possible even without social cohesion. Another example of this principle at work is the Chicago Bulls team, which dominated the NBA in the 1990s. The team members allegedly did not speak to each other off-court, but practised and competed together with 100% professionalism and commitment.

With this example in mind, Carron et al recently set up a new study to examine the relationship between task cohesion and team success in elite basketball and football teams[4], measuring just the group integration task and group attraction to task categories of cohesion from the GEQ. Each member of the 18 basketball and nine football teams involved tackled the following questions after the end of their regular season, ranking each answer from 1 ('strongly disagree') to 9 ('strongly agree'). Questions 1-4, 7 and 9 were reverse scored (ie 9 = 1)

1. I am not happy with the amount of influence I have.
2. I am unhappy with my team's level of desire to win.
3. This team does not give enough opportunities to improve my personal performance.
4. I do not like the technical strategy of this team.
5. Our team is united in trying to reach its goals for performance.
6. We all take responsibility for any loss or poor performance.
7. Our team members have conflicting aspirations for the team's performance.
8. If a team member has a problem, everyone wants to help him.
9. Our team members do not communicate freely about each player's responsibilities during competition and practice.

The key findings were as follows:

- The mean team cohesion scores for basketball teams were 6.05 for group integration task and 6.11 for attraction to group task. For football teams the mean scores were 6.33 and 7.04 respectively.
- Scores in both these categories were highly correlated with team success for both sports, success being defined as match results over the season, excluding play-offs. The teams with the highest 'team cohesion' scores had the best season win:loss percentage records.

This study offers clear evidence that real-world sports teams benefit from high levels of task cohesion. The strength of the relationship between cohesion, as measured by the task categories of the GEQ and team success as measured by the win:loss record was higher than in previous research. The researchers believe that this is because they focused on task cohesion using the GEQ, integrated individual scores to produce a team cohesion score and then related these scores to an indisputable measure of team success. All things considered, this study goes further than any before it to examine the importance of cohesion for success in team sports.

The implication of these findings is that coaches and sports psychologists would be well advised to assess team cohesion and develop team-building strategies to improve task cohesion. Specifically, coaches could work on making sure that team members are clear about and happy with team goals and the level of shared commitment. They could also work on developing team communication and shared responsibility – developing the 'we' mentality.

In his book on football psychology, Sven Goran Eriksson talks a great deal about how the 'we' mentality can raise the performance of all the players in a team and help reduce the pressure associated with big matches[5]. He describes eight key attributes of an effective team, and I invite you to note that all are task-oriented and have nothing to do with social relationships. The 'good team', according to the England manager, has:

1. a common vision
2. clear and definite goals which go hand in hand with this vision
3. members who share their understanding of strategy and tactics
4. great inner discipline (meaning they act professionally together)
5. players with characteristics which complement each other
6. a good division of roles among the players, with all members being treated equally
7. players who put the common good before their own interests
8. players who take responsibility for the whole team, with everyone accepting mistakes as long as people do their best.

Raphael Brandon

References

1. Lenk (1969) 'Top Performance Despite Internal Conflict'. In *Sport, Culture and Society: A reader on the Sociology of Sport,* Collier-Macmillan
2. *Psychological Bulletin* 115, pp210-227
3. *Journal of Sport Psychology* 7, pp244-266
4. *Journal of Sports Sciences* 20, pp119-126.
5. Sven Goran Eriksson (2000), *Sven Goran Eriksson on Football,* Carlton Books